KEY TIMES FOR PLAY

Debating Play Series ■

Series Editor: Tina Bruce

The intention behind the 'Debating Play' series is to encourage readers to reflect on their practice so that they are in a position to offer high quality play opportunities to children. The series will help those working with young children and their families in diverse ways and contexts, to think about how to cultivate early childhood play with rich learning potential.

The 'Debating Play' series examines cultural myths and taboos. It considers matters of human rights and progress towards inclusion in the right to play for children with complex needs. It looks at time-honoured practices and argues for the removal of constraints on emergent play. It challenges readers to be committed to promoting play opportunities for children traumatized through war, flight, violence and separation from loved ones. The series draws upon crucial contemporary research which demonstrates how children in different parts of the world develop their own play culture in ways which help them to make sense of their lives.

Published and forthcoming titles:
Holland: *We Don't Play With Guns Here*
Hyder: *War, Conflict and Play*
Kalliala: *Play Culture in a Changing World*
Orr: *My Right to Play: A Child with Complex Needs*

KEY TIMES FOR PLAY

The first three years

Julia Manning-Morton and Maggie Thorp

Open University Press
Maidenhead · Philadelphia

Open University Press
McGraw-Hill Education
McGraw-Hill House
Shoppenhangers Road
Maidenhead
Berkshire
England
SL6 2QL

email: enquiries@openup.co.uk
world wide web: www.openup.co.uk

and
325 Chestnut Street
Philadelphia, PA 19106, USA

First published 2003

A catalogue record of this book is available from the British Library

ISBN 0 335 21197 6 (pb)   0 335 21198 4 (hb)

Library of Congress Cataloging-in-Publication Data
CIP data applied for

Typeset by RefineCatch Limited, Bungay, Suffolk
Printed in Great Britain by Bell and Bain Ltd, Glasgow

CONTENTS

SERIES EDITOR'S PREFACE

The Debating Play series is not intended to make comfortable reading. This is because 'play' is not a comfortable subject. For a century at least, play has been hotly debated among researchers, practitioners, parents, politicians and policy makers. Arguments have centred around whether it should have a place in any childhood curriculum framework. Its presence in schools and other institutions and settings has ebbed and flowed according to who holds power, influence and authority to control curriculum decisions.

When play has been permitted in settings, it has often suffered from a work/play divide. Play in such contexts is frequently confused with recreation. However, an alternative approach is to offer 'free play', through which children are thought to learn naturally. This works well in mixed age groups (2–7 years) when older, more experienced child players act as tutors and initiate younger children, helping them to learn through their play. Sadly, though, this is rarely experienced in early childhood settings in the UK nowadays. It is noteworthy, however, that a few nursery schools have managed, against great odds, to keep an age range from 3–5 years. Research (Siraj-Blatchford *et al.* 2002) indicates that the learning that children do through their play in these settings is rich.

There is a growing understanding of the importance of play as diverse evidence accrues, which highlights the role of play in early learning in relation to ideas, feelings, relationships and movement (embodiment). However, this is often mistakenly interpreted as adults showing children how to play, through guiding, tutoring, role-modelling or whatever name is of current fashion, rather than providing children with genuine opportunities to engage in their *own* play.

The Debating Play series is evidence based rather than belief driven, and each book probes an aspect of play.

Julia Manning-Morton and Maggie Thorp have established a respected reputation for the quality of work they undertake in supporting practitioners and those taking further studies in relations to children up to three years of age. They have pioneered (in the London Borough of Camden) a course, 'Key Times: A framework for developing high quality provision for children under three'. This has proved to be of such benefit to those participating that it is now used widely in the national context, with great effect. It also contributed to the thinking of the working party, of which Julia Manning-Morton was a member, which developed for the DfES the document 'Birth to Three Matters'.

This book amplifies the importance of play for such young children, and explores its contribution to their development. It will help readers to deepen their understanding of play from the beginning, and to support parents and practitioners in cultivating it. The book will challenge readers to give children exciting environments, and give the sensitive adult the support they need if they are to play with quality.

This is a thought-provoking book, which is also very practical in its approach. It will help practitioners, or those training them, to find effective strategies for developing play so that it goes beyond being pedestrian – as is widespread in many settings. There is a strong message in this book, that although children may be very young, they appreciate, value and benefit from adults who help them to play. This book made me want to get started at once. Hopefully, this will be so for all who read it.

I commend this book to you.

Reference

Siraj-Blatchford, I., Sylva, K., Mittock, S., Gilden, R. and Bell, D. (2002) *Researching Effective Pedagogy in the Early Years*, Research Report 356, Department for Education and Skills

Tina Bruce

PREFACE

Julia Manning-Morton is a senior lecturer on the early childhood studies scheme at London Metropolitan University. Before going to work at the university she was an early years adviser in the London Borough of Camden and she has worked as a freelance trainer specializing in practice with children from birth to three.

Julia has worked as an early years practitioner and manager across a range of settings for children aged 0–8 years. She qualified as an NNEB in 1976 and completed an MA in Early Childhood Education with Care in 2000, throughout which she focused on the care and education of children from birth to 3 years old.

Maggie Thorp, until September 2001, was an early years adviser for Camden Local Education Authority, a freelance early years trainer specializing in practice with children from birth to three and a visiting lecturer at London Metropolitan University. She has now transferred to the early years directorate at Ofsted.

Maggie has extensive experience of working with children from birth to three and managing nurseries with baby and toddler rooms. This experience has been in community and local authority nurseries. She qualified as an NNEB in 1972 and went on to do an Advanced Diploma in Child Development at the Institute of Education in 1997.

We believe that our professional backgrounds and personal experiences give rise to the values that inform the writing of this book:

- that all young children must be listened to, respected and valued;
- that providing well for young children means thinking carefully about their concerns, interests and needs and about all aspects of

the provision; giving equal consideration to children's care and learning;

- that providing well for young children's emotional, personal and social development is a priority, which means focusing on what they are doing now rather than what we think they should be doing in the future;
- that the well-being of children cannot be separated from the well-being of the adults who care for them; therefore those adults must also be listened to, respected and valued;
- that the well-being of young children is the social responsibility of all, not just the private concern of parents and carers.

Julia and Maggie are joint authors of *Key Times: A Framework for Developing High Quality Provision for Children Under Three Years*. This document was the result of a two-year project undertaken with practitioners working with children from birth to three in early years settings in the London Borough of Camden. As such it arises from the practice wisdom of practitioners as well as the theoretical framework of researchers and academics. Many of the ideas in the *Key Times* framework document are reproduced in this book and, we hope, a synthesis of theory and practice is also reflected here.

Many of the observations and case study extracts used in the book were made by the authors and birth to threes practitioners during our research for the Key Times Framework (2001), several of them appear on the video that accompanies the framework document. Other examples are taken from observations the authors have made at home and in settings while studying the play, growth and learning of children from birth to three.

ACKNOWLEDGEMENTS

We would like to thank all the children, parents/carers and practitioners with whom we have worked over the years and whose words, photographs and ideas are part of this book.

As young practitioners we were both lucky enough to work with Elinor Goldschmied and would like to show our appreciation of her advocacy of good practice at that time as well as acknowledge her continuing influence on our approach today. We also appreciate the support and encouragement we have had at different times from Tina Bruce, Margy Whalley and Peter Elfer, for our approach and ideas and the translation of those into writing. We would also like to thank our recent and current colleagues in Camden, Ofsted and at London Metropolitan University for their support and understanding.

Most importantly we thank our partners, Dona and Wilf, for being the secure base from which we could venture out on this challenging adventure and to whom we could retreat when it became too overwhelming. And thank you to Billie for being a joy and for tolerating having a mother glued to a computer.

1

OUR CHANGING UNDERSTANDING OF CHILDREN FROM BIRTH TO THREE AND THEIR PLAY

The importance of context

In a busy group of children aged 6 months to 2 years old, Katherine sits on a low chair feeding Edie with her bottle. Twenty-two-month-old Melanie is sitting on a beanbag surrounded by books she has selected from the low open shelves, perused and then discarded. Tom (14 months) approaches Katherine and offers her a shaker to listen to, they talk about the sound it makes. When Edie has finished feeding, she and Hassan (8 months) sit in a protected corner of the room exploring a wealth of different objects in the Treasure Basket (Goldschmied and Jackson 1994), while Tom and three other mobile babies follow Max to the hall area, which has been prepared for their regular Heuristic Play session (Goldschmied and Jackson 1994). Melanie has now joined some toddlers from the neighbouring group in the shared passage area, crawling through the transparent tunnel into a tent and following the older toddlers up, down and around the slide. She can see Katherine, who is sitting attentively with Edie and Hassan, through the open, folding partition doors. She briefly returns to Katherine's side before zooming back out to bounce on the small trampoline with Kojo, while Wendy sings the Jumping Bean song to them.

Next door in a group of 2–3-year-olds Bethany is in the home area with a large cone hat on her head, scooping lentils from one of three shallow trays with a bottle top into a metal bowl. In the centre of the room Debbie sits with three children, each with a tray and tools, dripping gloop from their fingers.

'Ooh, it's drippy, cold and drippy', she says. The child on her lap gradually feels confident to dip his finger into the tray.

Across the room Mishka transfers some cars from the sand tray on a stand to the one on the floor in order that he can sit in the tray and run the cars along the track he has made. Marilyn, his key worker follows him, explaining to a disconcerted Robert what Mishka is doing so that they can continue to play together, encouraging Robert to find more cars in the container next to the tray.

Three children are experimenting with launching small toy aeroplanes into the air. 'How can we fly our planes so that they don't crash onto us?' wonders Corinne. Together they find thin cardboard tubes and pieces of card to which they tape their vehicles. Over the course of the day most of the children join in with this idea and can be seen moving around the room 'flying' their aeroplanes over their heads. Some of the children who have finished exploring the gloop decide to go out in the rain. They put on boots and jackets and take a small umbrella each from the crate by the door and go out to splash in puddles with Marcia. Mishka follows but not before balancing along the planks set out on low blocks in the passageway.

(Key Times Video 2001)

This observation is full of rich, appropriate play experiences for children from birth to three but many of those who work with babies and toddlers wrestle with what the role of play is for very young children. Practitioners struggle to respond appropriately to pressure to bring their curriculum in line with that of the curriculum for the foundation stage (QCA/DfEE 2000) for older children, and to have clear learning objectives, while continuing to provide good quality, age-appropriate play experiences. This difficulty is now being recognized and local initiatives such as the Key Times Framework (Manning-Morton and Thorp 2001) and national guidance in the form of *Birth to Three Matters* (Sure Start 2002) are in place to support practitioners working with babies and toddlers.

Such recognition and support is to be welcomed but it remains that how successfully practitioners provide for the play of children from birth to three will depend on:

- their knowledge of child development and of the historical, social and cultural contexts of developmental theory;
- their understanding of different perspectives on play;
- the relevance of those perspectives for children under three in

general and for the sociocultural experience of the particular children in their care;
• their knowledge of individual children, gleaned from frequent observations and from parent's wisdom.

When practitioners working with young children have a broad knowledge of child development theory and a deep understanding of the development of each individual child they can provide engaging play experiences and understand the processes and content of children's play, but throughout history and around the world, there have been and are, different ways of understanding children and childhood. It is therefore equally important for early years practitioners to understand the historical, social and cultural contexts in which we view young children's development, as this will enable them to define their professional values.

Historical perspectives on babies and toddlers

Babies, it seems have not been seen as people at all. The word infancy means 'without speech' and it is this element of not having speech that, until recently, has limited (scientific) understanding of babies' capabilities. For centuries it was thought that babies couldn't think, reason or know because we could not ask them or remember our own babyhood. An extreme example of the result of this view is that until recently some kinds of operations on newborn babies would be performed without an anaesthetic (Gopnik *et al.* 1999).

It used to be thought that a baby's experience was one of 'blooming, buzzing confusion' (William James in Gopnik *et al.* 1999: 65), a bombardment of sensory information of which the infant could make little sense. In addition babies have been seen as victims of their all-consuming emotional desires and as bundles of physical needs who have no sense of who they are and only a blurry sense of others. In this perspective babies are seen as acting only in response to innate physical and mental drives such as hunger and fear, and are passive in the process of their learning, moulded by their environment and adults around them.

Practice has, in the past, reflected this view, with practitioners seeing their role purely in relation to the children's physical needs. Physical and emotional needs were seen as needing to be trained so as not to run out of control and the child become dominant and demanding.

Toddlers in particular have been thought of as needing to be controlled and are still often discussed as if they are wild animals that need taming. Many descriptions of toddlers come from comparing them with older children, resulting in a negative, deficit view emphasizing what toddlers can't do or lack such as sharing or waiting.

Perspectives on play

In the following chapters we look in detail at different views of play and how they relate to babies and toddlers (see Bruner *et al.* 1976; Moyles 1989; Saracho and Spodek 1998; Garvey 1990). Broadly they are as follows:

Play as a means to let off steam and exercise muscles

This idea is often applied to children from birth to three whose physicality is central to their experience. The risk though of not understanding the full value of physical play is that it is then undervalued with practitioners making a false differentiation between 'play' (running about) and 'learning' (sitting down).

Play as a rehearsal for life in the future

Toddlers can often be seen imitating older children and adults in their play. Seeing this only as copying however, may lead practitioners to

It is important to understand the full value of physical play.

inhibit certain types of play as they think it may lead to undesirable character formation and so see their role as instructing the children in skills necessary for later on in life. They may see imitation as a sign of a toddler's lack of individual ideas.

Play as an expression of inner conflict

Even before they can talk children express both their joys and worries in their play. The danger is that practitioners, who have inadequate understanding of the child's context, can overinterpret what they observe. A balance is needed here, as with very young children signals of possibly serious problems may be subtler and more easily missed. Therefore continuity of carers and regular and frequent observation is important.

Play as a means for learning

Many early years specialists have written about children as constructors of their own learning, disseminating the theoretical ideas of Piaget and Vygotsky amongst early years practitioners (see, for example, Wood 1988). However, much of this writing has been focused on children over 3 years old. Despite the work of people such as Judy Dunn (1988), it is only with the more recent contributions of cognitive and neuroscience that the same kind of active learning is being attributed to babies and toddlers.

Children from birth to three do learn through their play; they learn about themselves, about others and about the world around them. In this view the adult's role is sometimes seen as necessarily intervening in the children's play in order to make it more educational (Saracho and Spodek 1998). The importance of the practitioner's role in the play of children from birth to three is not in dispute, however the risk of this view is that what is seen as educational is defined in too narrow terms and that children's play is appropriated by the adults who have their own agenda, possibly narrowing the scope of the children's experience. Play may only be seen as valuable when the adult can perceive the learning taking place and measure it in terms of outcomes. This of course is easier with skills such as naming colours and counting but possibly harder for the adult to identify learning such as an attitude of confidence in oneself or a disposition of empathy to others in distress (Katz 1988). As they grow babies and toddlers will have plenty of opportunity to learn the former but the foundation for the latter skills are laid in the first three years (Blakemore 1998; Siegal 1999).

The focus on children over 3 in writing about children's play has arisen partly from the artificial divide between 'education' and 'care' (and thereby over and under-3s) provision in Britain, with many studies of children's play taking place in nursery schools and classes catering predominantly for 3–5-year-olds. It has also arisen from our understanding of very early development. For example, the much emphasized and alleged egocentricity of toddlers has led to a view of them only playing alone or alongside others, unable to engage in cooperative pretend play (Parten 1932). Babies may engage in explorative play but this is seen as a process of taking in the properties of objects rather than thinking about them and making sense of their experience. Overall this results in many adults thinking that babies do not really play at all and toddlers do not play properly.

These views invite problems in nursery settings because expectations are not appropriate. Problems arise because babies are bored or because toddlers are in a baby room environment that may be limiting for them or they are offered a diluted programme for 3–5-year-olds that embodies expectations that result in frustration for the adults and children. The bad press that toddlers get for being egocentric, possessive, uncooperative, clinging, incomprehensible and for biting and having temper tantrums then becomes a self-fulfilling prophecy.

Of course babies and toddlers can show all these characteristics in their play, just as older children and adults can also show all these characteristics: dependent and independent, active and passive, rational and emotional, selfish and empathic, possessive and generous and everything in between these polarized states.

It is surprising that we need reminding of this continuum between infancy, childhood and adulthood. Maybe it is because in our vertically linear society with small, dispersed families, we tend to live our lives so separately; children, teenagers, adults and older people tend to occupy different and separate social spaces. For those adults who do live their lives alongside children, however, there has always been an element of understanding the connectedness of our adult being to our childlike states and childhood experiences. Gopnik *et al.* (1999) say that women have always known the complexities and capabilities of young children. It is only now that women and mothers are also scientists that such knowledge is being given scientific status.

The importance of the first three years of life

A key concept that science is offering us today is that the stimuli and experiences babies are exposed to enable the brain to lay down more and more connections or networks and that the first two or three years of life are important for developing a rich complex of connections. This period of life then may be seen as critical for learning, an idea that commercial companies have exploited by producing special flash cards or music tapes to speed up children's learning. This is not the approach advocated in this book. Gopnik *et al.* (1999) emphasize that what babies need is not extra input but the experiences of everyday life with their close adults and peers. It is also important to remember that the door on development does not slam shut at age 3. Brain development continues throughout early childhood and there is another significant burst of brain activity in the teenage years (Carter 1999). However psychoanalytic theory has always suggested, and neuroscience is now also showing us, that all of a child's early experiences, whether remembered or forgotten, will influence their later development considerably (Eliot 1999; Siegel 1999). In the light of the rapidity of children's development between the ages of 0 and 3 years and the impact of the environment on their future development, the quality of the services they receive, the play opportunities they have and, most importantly, the calibre of the people who look after them can be seen as crucial.

Anne Meade said that 'Children are the messages to a time we will never see' (Meade 1995). By the same token adults are messages from the past. This does not separate us from each other – rather it brings us

All of a child's early experiences will influence their later development considerably.

together. As children grow up to be adults alongside us we share our lives and the world together. They will be the nurse or doctor doing our hip replacements or the tax inspector assessing our returns in later life. How gentle, understanding and fair they are will be influenced by the relationships we have with them now.

Current perspectives on development and play

The authors have found it helpful in their work to think in terms of a continuum of development through life and also to think of the children in terms of their key characteristics. We find that it ensures that we think of children from birth to three as individual people with their own unique characteristics as well as those they share with others. This emphasizes a holistic approach to play for children from birth to three. We believe that quality play experiences are those that are based on the characteristics and interests of this age group rather than on artificially divided areas of learning or development. This is the approach taken by the London Borough of Camden Under Threes Development Group when developing *Key Times: A Framework for Developing High Quality Provision for Children under Three Years* (Manning-Morton and Thorp 2001), in which we explore effective practice in relation to eight key characteristics of babies and toddlers.

Birth to Three Matters (Sure Start 2002) also focuses on components such as 'A Strong Child', 'An Effective Communicator' and 'A Healthy Child', reflecting the understanding of those who have worked with this age group for many years, that a watered down 3–5s curriculum is not appropriate for children up to 3 years old.

In the first three years of life changes take place more rapidly than at any other time

Our increasing knowledge of the development of infants and toddlers has led to a greater appreciation of the complexity and rapidity of development in the first three years of life. This is particularly true in relation to brain development where the connections between neural cells are sparse at birth but are made at a terrific rate until they reach maximum density at age 6 (Carter 1999). From birth the infant actively seeks and uses stimulation in order for unfinished connections to be strengthened and extended. It is the stimuli and experiences the baby is exposed to that enable the brain to lay down more connections, to prune unused or unnecessary ones and to strengthen

*The more varied and appropriate the experience, the better the
essential connections between neural cells in the brain.*

connections where experiences are repeated. Everything a baby
hears, sees, tastes, touches and smells, and all of a baby's movements
influence the way the brain makes its connections; the more varied
and appropriate the experience, the better the essential connections
between neural cells.

Movers and doers: The developing brain and maturing muscles of the
infant result in babies quickly gaining mobility. The rapid growth
and gaining of muscular strength in the first year of life, aided by
the physical play opportunities they have, enables young children
to change very quickly from immobile infants to running, jumping,
climbing toddlers who are constantly on the go.

Communicators: Babies are communicators from birth; they ensure
that their needs are met through a wide range of communication
strategies. In the second year of life there is an explosion of language yet toddlers still have a limited vocabulary, which is very
frustrating for them when they are trying to express themselves.
But when adults consider the rapid development from communicating through crying, gazing and body movements, to being able
to use short sentences, they appreciate what babies and toddlers can
do rather than what they cannot yet do. As practitioners observe
them at play they can become adept at reading these non-verbal
communications.

Social beings: Babies are interested in others from birth. Although they are attached to a few key people, who they are likely to feel most confident playing with at first, we can see how the social world of the new baby rapidly spreads outside the family to the community, thereby expanding friendships and an understanding of self and others. A baby goes from almost total self-centredness to the self-control and empathy of a 3-year-old in three short years.

Discoverers and explorers: Children from birth to three go from experiencing everything as new and strange – which is sometimes exciting but also sometimes scary – to having an understanding of cause and effect and using symbols in less than three years. Although toddlers are learning rapidly through their play and can sometimes appear wise beyond their years, it is often difficult for them to apply their new knowledge to new and different situations and so can show a surprising lack of understanding; the social understanding of what is acceptable and unacceptable is still being learned.

The rapidity of children's development between the ages of birth and three means that play experiences need to be varied yet also repeated, new yet also predictable. They need to be closely matched to the child's current skills, abilities and interests, yet offer sufficient challenge. Play opportunities offered should therefore arise from frequent observations by adults who know the children well.

In the first three years of life all areas of development are intertwined

In further developing their knowledge of the development of children from birth to three, practitioners may also increase their understanding of the interconnectedness of all aspects of development. They are then more able to consciously plan play experiences that are flexible and open ended, thereby supporting the children's development holistically.

Information gained from studies of the development and functioning of the brain help us to see how the physical development of the brain relates not only to children's cognitive and physical development but also to their emotional and social development. For example, we experience our feelings through the workings of the limbic system in the brain, which is closely connected to all areas of the cerebral cortex, which is why all our thoughts are imbued with feeling (Goleman 1996).

A child's physical development impacts on all other areas of development. Degrees of mobility and dexterity will determine the

*0–3 year olds need to be allowed to use play
experiences in a range of ways.*

kinds of experiences a child has. The way a child looks will influence
others' responses to them and therefore their social and emotional
relationships and their self-concept (Bee 2000).

The quality of a child's attachments to their close carers not only
affects their emotional development but their cognitive development. For example high levels of stress caused by repeated neglectful
or abusive experiences creates high levels of cortisol in young children's brains. Cortisol at too high a level can destroy brain cells and
weaken connections, thereby reducing the capacity to learn (Eliot
1999).

A child's ability to communicate with others will impact on the
degree to which they are able to get their needs met, their ability to
make friends and to contribute to a group. It will also impact on how
others will see them, especially views of their intelligence, all of which
will impact on the child's sense of self (Bee 2000).

The close intertwining of early development requires that play experiences can be used by the child in a range of ways. When planning play experiences, practitioners should ensure that the social and emotional aspects of play are considered as well as the physical, cognitive and linguistic aspects; they need to consider the dispositions children are developing as well as the skills and knowledge they may gain.

In the first three years of life children are dependent on adults to meet their needs

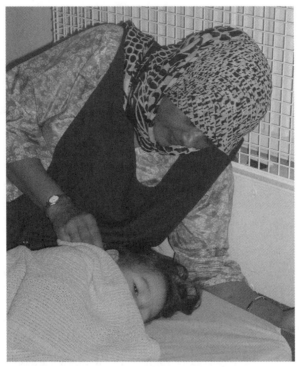

Children's physical and emotional dependence demands sensitive responses from a key person who knows them well.

Babies' physical dependence, such as needing feeding and changing, is closely intertwined with their emotional dependence. Babies need comforting, holding and protecting, reflecting their vulnerability and the intensity and immediacy of their needs. This physical dependence requires that practitioners be very aware of how they handle young children. Children's emotional dependence demands prompt responses and sensitive interactions with a key person who knows them well (Elfer *et al.* 2002; Manning-Morton and Thorp 2000, 2001). Their dependency is reflected in the amount of time they spend in physical care routines, when playing with experiences of dependency and independence are central. Therefore planning to use these routine times as creatively as possible and seeing them as opportunities for play is essential. Babies' physical dependence also means that for much of the first year of life they need us to bring the world to them and them to the world. A baby carried around in a sling or back carrier will see things from a different perspective and may encounter more people than a baby in a playpen.

Mobile babies and toddlers are beginning to experiment with physical and emotional independence. This is both exciting and frightening for the child who needs adults who will both support them in their explorations and also comfort them in times of stress.

The physical and emotional dependency of children from birth to three means that the relationship between the practitioner and the child is a central feature of any play experience. The practitioner's availability will influence the child's confidence in playing and as the adult is frequently the child's play object, practitioners need to ensure that they are available to the children for prolonged periods of time.

In the first three years of life children are establishing a sense of self

Children from birth to three are developing their self-concept, which is formed in their relationships with the people who are close to them.

Babies and toddlers developing self-concept influences their approach to playing.

Their self-concept influences their approach to playing and making relationships with others, to understanding others in their play, to finding out about the world and to life in the future.

A good self-concept largely comes from knowing those closest to you are on your side. If the children in nursery settings experience their practitioners as being on their side, willing them to succeed, supporting them through this challenging time, they will dare to take risks, to experiment and not be afraid to get things wrong. They will grow up to be socially competent players, confident learners with good self-esteem, able to cooperate and appreciate each other in their play.

Neuroscience also suggests that between the ages of 1½ and 2½ years brain development reflects this emergence of personhood (Blakemore 1998; Siegel 1999). Therefore if the first three years are especially sensitive for learning, it is in relation to emotional security and social relationships. Hot-housing intellectual development is more likely to result in children adopting negative dispositions to learning rather than making lasting cognitive gains.

Play experiences should therefore positively reflect and value each child's identity and background and have children's social relationships as a central focus in which the practitioner supports the interactions between children.

The importance of developing high quality contexts for play

It is important that adults who are significant in the lives of young children think about why play is important in the lives of babies and toddlers. To do this they first need to understand what children from birth to three are like and therefore what kind of play experiences they will enjoy. Then they should reflect on how to provide appropriate contexts in which babies and toddlers will want to play.

The cornerstone of high quality play provision for children from birth to three is the quality of their relationships with their key persons. Therefore they require highly skilled and committed practitioners who are able to:

- act as guides and supporters to our youngest children;
- work closely with parents and carers in sharing knowledge of their children's play;
- respond well to the children's emotional, social, physical, communication and cognitive needs in their chosen play scenarios;

The conerstone of high quality play provision for 0–3 year olds is the quality of their relationship with their key person.

- provide appropriately for their play through the quality of their relationships and the physical and psychological environment they provide.

Each of these aspects is explored throughout the rest of this book as babies and toddlers learn through all of their play experiences with adults and other children as well as with objects, and they do not divide their day into playing time and other times. Therefore planning for the play of children from birth to three must include all times of the day and all aspects of the curriculum, including the practitioner's role (Manning-Morton and Thorp 2001).

An overriding focus of developing high quality contexts must be attention to the fine detail of all aspects of provision for babies and toddlers. Statements of intent, such as those above, may at first seem straightforward but it is only in discussing the detail of what we mean by 'work closely with . . .' or 'respond well to . . .' that we can come to a shared vision of what we mean by these aspects of quality. The detail of how we feed a baby, the passageway between in and outdoors or how we present an opportunity to explore cornflour, will impact for better or worse on the children's play, growth and learning.

A 'key times' perspective on play for children from birth to three

Each of the points outlined above and explored in later chapters may be summarized as the following principles:

- High quality play for children from birth to three derives from the practitioner's knowledge and understanding of theories of play and development, from reflection on their own experiences and values and from detailed observation of individual children.
- High quality play for children from birth to three takes place in a context of:

  - a secure relationship between key person and child,
  - shared care between parents/carers and practitioners,
  - high levels of communication and support between practitioners,
  - well thought-out routine care times,
  - an appropriately designed and prepared environment.

- High quality play for children from birth to three is planned across all aspects of the provision with attention to the detail of how play experiences are presented and supported.

Throughout this book the personal, social and emotional aspects of children's play are emphasized. This is because we believe these aspects to underpin children's positive use of play in all other domains. It is as if babies and toddlers use play as a mirror in which to see themselves from different perspectives and ask questions such as 'Who am I?', 'How does my body work?' and 'Who might I be?' They also use play as a kind of ticket to the social life of the community where they explore questions of 'Who are you?', 'How are we the same and different?' and 'What can we do together?' But of course we also see children from birth to three using play as a tool with which they are making sense of the world and how it works. They are solving questions of 'What is it?', 'What does it do?' and 'What can I do with it?'

2

CHILDREN FROM BIRTH TO THREE PLAYING, GROWING AND LEARNING THROUGH THEIR CLOSE RELATIONSHIPS

Developing an emotional context that supports play

Nena (14 months old) approaches the water tray where Graham, her key person, is crouched playing with two other children. She is tearful and sucking her thumb. As she approaches, Graham looks up at her saying, 'Nena's got another dress on, blue and white stripes.' She stands next to him still with her thumb in her mouth. He shows her the water while comfortingly holding one hand on her back. Another child needs help and Graham goes over to him; Nena starts crying. Graham comes back to her. 'Its all right, Nena, what's the matter?' He crouches down and asks her if she wants some juice. She cries when he stands up to take it from the shelf. Nena rejects the juice even after Graham offers the cup in different ways, so he tries to interest her in the water again. She watches with her thumb in her mouth, then half-heartedly takes a bottle of water with which to pour but drops it. She cries and Graham, still crouching down, takes her on his knee.

Although his co-worker is supportively looking after the rest of the children, Graham needs to see to another child. Nena cries again, slightly louder. He picks her up and offers her juice again; she shakes her head. 'Do you want to go to bed?' He asks. She nods in agreement so Graham sits to one side of the room gently rocking her in his arms and singing quietly while she drops off to sleep.

(Key Times Video 2001)

Physical and emotional dependency

This observation illustrates the immediacy and fluctuating nature of babies' and toddlers' physical and emotional needs and the effect of this on their play. It is clear that babies' and toddlers' physical dependence means that they are very vulnerable, as they are totally reliant on someone else to satisfy their physical needs and therefore to help them to survive (Manning-Morton and Thorp 2001) but it is important to understand how their physical dependence is closely intertwined with their emotional dependence. An obvious illustration of this is of food and feeding. When we feed a baby we are not only offering them nutrients but also nurturing, we show our love and care through responding to a child's cries of hunger and the baby links the experience of having their discomfort eased with their close adult's gentle touch and soothing voice. We are aware of this link throughout our lives; we cook for or take our loved ones out for dinner, we 'comfort eat' or are 'off our food' in times of distress. How important then that practitioners understand and are alert to the strong links between physical and emotional experiences in early childhood.

Lise Eliot (1999) describes how the development of the somato-sensory (of the body and the senses) system of the brain through touch is important not only for moulding later tactile sensitivity, motor skills and understanding of the physical world but also for good health and emotional well-being. Therefore meeting children's physical needs only is not sufficient; children do not thrive if they do not also receive loving attention. In the observation above we can see how Nena's key person effectively provides this attention with his voice, his body language and gestures. His gentle rocking of Nena clearly tells her that her needs are important and deserving of a caring response. He understands that her ability to play is diminished when she is distressed.

All of a child's early experiences, whether remembered or forgotten, will influence their later development considerably (Eliot 1999; Siegel 1999), particularly the emotional learning that takes place in their relationships with the adults and children to whom they are close. For this reason, the relationship between the adult and child must be given due attention when developing good quality play experiences. Through their interactive experiences children build up a mental model of the world in which the self and significant others and their interrelationships are represented. Babies and toddlers use this mental model to recreate and predict relationships with others; John Bowlby called this an 'Internal Working Model' (1969; 110–15). In play and at physical care times, babies are learning about their emotions, how they affect others and within that relationship, how to regulate their emotions and act in socially acceptable ways. For example, at 10 months old Billie knew that by wrinkling up her nose and snuffling, she could make her childminder's older children laugh.

First relationships and play

Responsiveness and attunement (Stern 1990) are the necessary key characteristics of practitioners in supporting children's emotional learning. It is in rapid, regulated, face-to-face interactions that the attuned caregiver not only minimizes the infant's negative feelings but also maximizes their positive affective states (Schore 2001). Therefore young children require responsive practitioners who will play with and comfort them in the way that is most helpful to them as an individual at that particular time.

Young children are very dependent on adults for comfort. They need to spend a lot of time being held, rocked and gently stroked as they experience their physical feelings with great intensity. For an infant the intensity of their feelings gives rise to their first feelings of anxiety. If babies' needs are not responded to they cannot find a causal connection between needing and receiving. Anxiety then mounts that this discomfort will go on forever and they have two

In sensitive, attuned interactions the baby's positive affective states will be maximized.

options, to disintegrate into frantic crying or to withdraw into despairing sleep (Lieberman 1993). In this context babies are learning that the world is an untrustworthy place, threatening to their sense of well-being and is to be approached with caution. They are also learning to expect little from close relationships and receiving negative messages about their worth as a person. Children's curiosity and ability to play may then be impaired (Creasey *et al.* 1998).

On the other hand babies who have repeated experiences of loving responses to their signals learn that discomfort does not last forever, to wait with hope, and are gradually able to manage the anxiety, because their parent or practitioner manages it for them. Babies then learn that the world is a benevolent place worthy of being explored, that people can be trusted and therefore the babies themselves can be trusting and trusted and believe in themselves (Lieberman 1993). In this way, physical and emotional interactions between the adult and child that are consistent and that offer constancy and continuity of experience, are internalized by the child who can then develop an integrated, continuous sense of self (Bain and Barnet 1980). Creasey *et al.* (1998) describe how this then contributes to a child's social competence, which in turn affects their ability to engage in social play.

Emotional holding

The high level of empathy required by very young children is described in psychoanalytic terms as 'container–contained' (Shuttleworth in Miller *et al.* 1989: 28). Judy Shuttleworth (1989) describes the way in which a mother is able to get in contact with her baby's state of mind as a relationship in which the mother's mind acts as a container for the baby. In this way the mother holds the baby's distressed and uncomfortable feelings in her mind, which would otherwise feel to the baby as if they were falling apart. By developing a similar level of empathic response, practitioners can also provide effective emotional holding for their key children.

The authors have sometimes likened the idea of containment to the role a seat belt plays. It is loose and flexible enough to allow for ordinary movement but in an emergency holds you to prevent you getting hurt. An infant's need for this particular sort of adult emotional holding and receptivity from adults continues in varying degrees as children grow up and as they have periods of greater or lesser fragility. In early years settings, even babies or toddlers who have been attending the group for some time have periods of being unsettled. They can cling, needing a lot of holding when they are

Children's ability to play is diminished when tired, upset or unwell.

tired, unwell or upset by events in their lives and their health can fluctuate rapidly, causing changes in their mood and sense of well-being. Their ability to play is greatly diminished when in these states. This is clear in the earlier observation of Nena, who, although usually well settled and enthusiastic in her play, was developing a cold and was unable to participate in the water play at all.

Attachment and play

Bowlby (1969) describes how maintaining the equilibrium of the relationship between adult and child, through being caring, sensitive, available and responsive, allows the child to develop an attachment relationship with the adult. Children who have secure attachment relationships are more able to be independent, to relate to their peers and engage in more complex and creative play. Such children are more flexible and resourceful and have higher self-esteem (Schaffer and Emerson 1964).

Staying near

Seeking proximity to an adult is a key feature of an attachment relationship. Babies and toddlers show their need to feel secure through searching for their carer when they are not in sight, reaching up to be picked up, cuddling and clinging, and following or approaching their key person. These behaviours can frequently be observed in babies' and toddlers' play. The distance at which the child feels comfortable will depend on factors such as age, temperament, developmental history, and whether the child feels tired, frightened or ill, as we saw in the observation earlier when Nena cried each time her key person moved away. Recent separation will lead to greater proximity seeking and the degree of proximity will depend on circumstances such as the familiarity of the environment (Holmes 1993).

These behaviours start to become apparent around the time babies become mobile. They begin to show distress when strangers come into the room and cling to their parent or key person, refusing to go to people they do not know well. This 'stranger anxiety' (Ainsworth *et al.* 1978) shows us that the child is clearly differentiating between people they know and has a relationship with and those they do not. When first visiting an early years setting or any unfamiliar place, babies and toddlers are more likely to play by exploring their environment, interacting with other adults and showing interest in other children while their parents/carers are close by.

Separation and loss

The other side of the attachment coin is loss. Having to be without people we are close to is not easy, even when we have the mature understanding of an adult. The process of loss experienced by young children on separation has been likened to the same process that adults experience on bereavement or perhaps divorce (Bowlby 1979). This can help practitioners understand that a child will go through phases of protest, withdrawal and detachment from play and from people and that these phases will include aspects of grief such as yearning, searching, anger, and despair (Robertson and Robertson 1953).

The primary response produced in children by separation from the attachment figure is protest. Babies and toddlers express their distress about having to be without their parents/carers through crying, screaming and kicking, shouting and biting. Bowlby emphasized that these were normal responses to a threat to an attachment bond that needed to be understood and supported rather than condemned or suppressed (1973: Ch. 1).

After the initial protest children may quieten, a phase that might be interpreted as the child becoming more settled. However close observation may reveal that they are more likely to have become withdrawn and detached. A child in this state will not readily play with people or objects, they will not explore their environment with any interest or enthusiasm and will no longer assert their needs. They may be observed to sit staring into the middle distance as if they are in reverie or tuned out. A child in this state is unable to play wholeheartedly, therefore a fundamental concern for supporting young children's play must be the development of a close relationship with an identified key person; a relationship that is built up gradually while the child is still supported by the presence of their parent or primary carer. Babies and toddlers who have this kind of relationship with their key person seem to trust the people around them and to be more confident in their exploratory and social play in the group.

Secure base

It is frequently said by practitioners that if they allow children to become attached to them it encourages dependence when what children need to learn is independence. There are two issues here. First, ideas of independence as a desirable state in a 1 or 2-year-old will vary according to historical and cultural contexts and may be heavily influenced by the adult's need for the child to be independent such as when caring for many children at once. Second, it is the emotional learning that happens in a close relationship that enables the child to develop the confidence to venture out to explore the world and make further close relationships.

This is called the secure base effect (Bowlby 1988), another key feature of attachment relationships. To create a secure base for a child is to create an ambience that supports the child in their task of integrating their need to feel safe in the protected sphere of intimate relationships with their need for carefree unrestricted exploration.

Children manifest specific behaviours in their play that enable practitioners to understand what the child wants or needs at any given time. For example, searching, reaching up, hugging, cuddling, clinging, approaching and following will indicate the need to feel secure. Looking out and pointing, crawling away, climbing, running, jumping and hiding show confidence in exploring. As babies' and toddlers' needs fluctuate in a short space of time so do these behaviours. They have busy periods where they follow their curiosity, but often need to retreat into the arms of their key person.

Mental health, resilience and well-being

The security of an early attachment relationship forms the basis of the child's future relationships, their social competence and their ability to engage in social play (Creasey et al. 1998). Bowlby (1965) saw prolonged separation and loss of the attachment relationship between mother and child as a prime determinant of unhappiness and disturbance. It is important to remember however, that there are many pathways through childhood and the influences of the child's own temperament, the extended family, friendships and success at school all play a part in different outcomes.

In the list of elements that define children's mental health, the Mental Health Foundation includes 'the ability to play and learn' (1999: 6). They list many factors that put a child's mental health at risk but also point out that some children, apparently against the odds, develop into 'competent, confident and caring adults' (Mental Health Foundation 1999: 9). They say that establishing a secure attachment in the first year of life is fundamental but there are other protective factors that may combine to enable children to be resilient. In the individual child these factors include temperament and intelligence. Factors in the family include the presence of substitute parents and positive role models; factors in the community include good quality childcare provision.

Sebastian Kraemer (1999) also describes how children who have been disadvantaged through early loss or abuse are often able to overcome their disadvantage through having had a 'champion' in their lives who respected them and in whom they could confide. Through the support of these later relationships children are able to develop the kind of resilience in life that is not resistant, tough, or about 'compulsive self-reliance' (Bowlby 1979: 138) but is about flexibility, being able to make sense of early experiences, being able to ask for help when needed and being able to put oneself in other people's shoes, all of which can be explored through play.

Ferre Laevers describes children, who are in a state of well-being, as feeling like 'fish in water' (Laevers et al. 1997: 15). They adopt an open, receptive and flexible attitude towards their environment. They have confidence and good self-esteem, as well as a big portion of fighting spirit. They radiate vitality and have fun with others (Laevers et al. 1997). The optimal way for a child to develop the kind of resilience that promotes their physical and mental well-being is through her or his earliest relationships with adults who are responsive, attentive and in tune with their needs (Kraemer 1999). Therefore, far from meaning that resilience or the influence of later experiences render the early years unimportant, they clearly indicate that the practitioner working with children from birth to three has an important role in developing close, key person relationships.

Play and feelings ▪

> At 18 months old, Billie had a bad fall and broke her front teeth. At the time this meant that she could not suck on her bottle and two months later had to have an operation to remove her damaged teeth. Before the operation the nursery lent her parents a small world set depicting a dentist's surgery. Before the operation Billie's mum used the set to introduce the idea of the dentist. When referring to her poorly teeth Billie would shake her head, look sad and say, 'No bot-bot'. After the operation they spent much time playing with the set; Billie would lead the play, covering the child doll's face and saying 'yuck'. The anaesthetic mask and smell of the gas was the most upsetting and frequently referred to part of the experience, which she would also re-play by covering her parents' faces with various objects and pressing down hard. Her broken teeth were kept in a special box that she would ask for and sit and talk about, frequently at first and gradually less frequently over the next two to three years. At this time similar smells to the gas would prompt her to recall the experience and look at her teeth. Billie did not give up her nighttime 'bot-bot' until she was 4. At 8 years old Billie wrote a story at school and like many authors used real life experience as her inspiration. The story was about a girl who has an accident and breaks her teeth and so could not suck on her bottle and has to have an anaesthetic. It ends 'but it all got better in the end'.

The significance of emotional learning in the first three years of life means that practitioners need a good understanding of how play can be a vehicle for expressing feelings and also a tool for making sense of and integrating children's emotional experiences.

The influence of psychoanalytic theory

One idea about children's play is that it allows the child to release or express their feelings. Melanie Klein describes how children express their phantasies, wishes and actual experiences in a symbolic way through play and games (1932).

In terms of emotional health and well-being, most early years practitioners would have great concern on observing a child who did not engage in play. This view has long been held in the early years tradition. Susan Isaacs regarded play as essential for the healthy emotional growth of children and saw the absence of play as a symptom of mental ill health (1929). For Winnicott play facilitates growth and therefore health; it is a form of communication and leads into group relationships; play is relational and therefore implies trust, it involves doing and therefore involves the body and taking time and play is essentially satisfying (1971).

Winnicott describes how the baby's playground is the (mental) space between the mother (or substitute) and the baby and that this is what makes it both exciting and potentially anxiety-provoking. In their interactions the baby is making explicit its internal reality, that is the degree of constancy and reliability of the adult the baby has internalized. In so doing the baby experiences the external reality of the adult's responses (1971). The degree of synchrony or attunement in these interactions affects the child's early emotional learning. For example, when a baby averts their gaze to avoid becoming overwhelmed in a game of bouncing on the knee, the adult needs to synchronize their disengagement. In this way baby and adult co-create interactive play that is a series of well-matched crescendos and decrescendos of emotional expression (Schore 2001).

Transitional objects

Where a baby has had substantial experience of synchrony, they are able to withstand minor experiences of asynchrony, such as needing feeding while still five minutes away from home in the car. This opens up a mental space between the baby and adult, in which the child may suck on their fists or the corner of a blanket, which Winnicott calls 'transitional phenomena or objects' (Winnicott 1971: Ch. 1). For the child they represent the stage of transition from the child feeling merged with their mother to seeing her as separate.

The use of transitional objects continues as children grow older. Many young children have a particular special toy or object that they carry around with them. This teddy, piece of cloth or whatever it may be, is imbued with 'motherness' and helps the child to recall a sense of comfort and security at times of stress. The smell and feel of the object is really important, as is its availability. To wash it or put it away until home time is to deprive the child of what Winnicott calls 'the first thing in the world that belongs to the infant, and yet is not part of the infant' (1957: 167) and 'the beginning of the infant's creation of

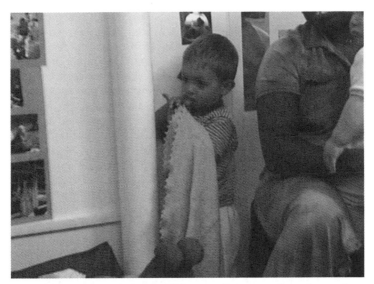

A transitional object helps a child to recall a sense of comfort and security at times of stress.

the world' (1957: 169). As the child manipulates the object, they invest it with their own meaning and feeling.

For Winnicott this is the beginning of a child's ability to play and that it is only in play that children and adults are able to be creative, not in the sense of producing works of art but in terms of being able to use the whole of our personality and discover the self (1971).

Play as therapy

It is in the emotional aspect of human development that we can see the historical links between psychoanalytic and educational disciplines, between emotional care and intellectual learning. Susan Isaacs was psychoanalytically trained in the Kleinian tradition and also ran the Malting House School in Cambridge. Anna Freud ran the Jackson Nursery in Vienna and the Hampstead War Nursery in London (later the Anna Freud Nursery School that closed in 1999). She was introduced to psychoanalysis by her father Sigmund Freud, trained as a teacher and also took courses in psychoanalysis (Young-Bruehl 1988).

These links have diminished in recent years and different emphases have grown up in their place. As Winnicott says: 'the teacher aims at enrichment. By contrast the therapist is concerned specifically with the child's own growth processes' (1971: 50). This marks a divergence between ideas of play: whether play is important for children's learning and later education or as a healing, integrative process that is spontaneous. In the former approach it is the adult's expected role to 'scaffold' (Bruner *et al.* 1976) the child's play. In the latter approach the adult must be available in case the play becomes overwhelming but not necessarily involved as a play partner. In the play as therapy perspective, it is the adult's role to allow time and space for the child's as yet unformed ideas to take shape and be expressed in their own way.

In child psychoanalysis play is the child's talk and forms the basis of play therapy. Here the child's play is self-directed but takes place within a protected, uninterrupted time and space, with the nondirective but full reflective attention of the adult. Axline (1964) gives a classic example of this process; practitioners with a social care background may be familiar with these concepts and provide 'special time' for children with particular difficulties.

Linnet McMahon (1994) points out that it may be sufficient for a child to have access to play opportunities in order to replay their experiences, play out their fears and be autonomous and creative in the safe context of play where they are in control and mistakes do not have serious consequences. However it is also useful for children to have their actions and feelings reflected back to them in a warm, accepting, genuine and empathic way. Naming and talking to children about feelings is rare; as practitioners we are often more intent on naming objects and their properties, particularly with boys. In order to effectively support babies' and toddlers' play it is useful for practitioners to develop reflective listening skills that follow the child's lead, are attentive and avoid questioning. For children from birth to three it is useful for practitioners to provide a running commentary on the child's play and to draw attention to the emotional and relational aspects of play.

Implications for practice

Ideas of the importance of self-directed play have on occasion been diluted and misused by practitioners as an excuse not to be involved in the children's play at all, either as observers or participants, saying that 'the children just need free play'. This is not true to a play as therapy approach. Winnicott says that children play more easily when the adult is able and free to play (1971).

In both the Malting House School and the Hampstead Nursery

the principle of closely observing children's play in order to better understand their thoughts and feelings was firmly established and the provision of play opportunities was carefully thought about. In the psychoanalytic tradition, the staff in these settings would have been aware of the danger of 'projecting' their own feelings onto the children and also of the effect of 'transference' whereby the adult's feelings may reflect the child's. Therefore observations were discussed between the staff in order to ensure unbiased interpretation (Young-Bruehl 1988).

This continues to be good practice today and it is also useful for practitioners to look at observations from different disciplinary perspectives, which is where working in a multidisciplinary team can be useful. For example: An observation of a child who is interested in tying string or tape between furniture or who repeatedly brings and collects objects to and from an adult, can be interpreted from a cognitive development perspective as the child exploring a connection schema (see Athey 1990; Bruce 1997). From a psychoanalytical perspective this child may be expressing a fear of separation and using string to stay connected on an emotional level (Winnicott 1971: 17). These interpretations will, of course be informed by the parents' perspective and information and other observations that provide a context for the child's behaviour.

The role of the adult in supporting play by developing close relationships

Developing an understanding of theories of emotional development and being able to identify the key features of attachment relationships enables early years practitioners to do the following:

- develop appropriate close relationships with children;
- work effectively with parents in sharing the care of their children;
- devise play experiences that support children's understanding of feelings and relationships;
- engage in play activities sensitively.

To understand the importance of their role at an emotional as well as an intellectual level it is useful for practitioners to reflect on their experiences in adult relationships. When asked to consider the positive elements of their close adult relationships, practitioners have previously suggested elements such as 'non-judgemental', 'listening and understanding', 'sharing and communicating', 'being there – investing time', 'supportive and pleased about achievements', 'hugs, cuddles and kindness' as positive features of close relationships. All these, they agreed, resulted in them feeling accepted – of both their good and bad sides, free to be themselves, more self-confident, loved and able to go out and conquer mountains (Manning-Morton 2000b). These are the sorts of relationships it is essential to build with children up to 3, to foster their development of a positive self-concept and their ability to play. To do this they need constancy of carers and continuity of care.

Key working and key person relationships

Studies of daycare settings in the 1970s and 80s (Bain and Barnett 1980; Marshall 1982; Belsky 1988) highlighted the inconsistent care babies received and led to greater awareness of the need for babies to have individualized care, thereby introducing the idea of key working. This concept, whereby a small group of children is assigned to be the primary responsibility of one adult, is the most effective way of ensuring that young children have their individual needs met in groups.

The aim of key working is to encourage the development of securely attached relationships between a child and their key person in

The aim of key working is to encourage the development of close relationships.

order to meet the emotional needs of the children. Young children can form attachments to a small number of people (Goosens and Van Ijzendoorn 1990; Rutter 1995) but this does not mean that they can easily bear the coming and going and multiple handling of several practitioners. On the contrary, it demands that practitioners pay attention to the quality of their key person relationship as an important person in that child's family of significant people. Helen Raikes (1993) points out that the longer the duration of the relationship between practitioner and child, the more attuned the practitioner is to the child and the more appropriate are the play opportunities.

When relating the key working concept to young children's play it is important to distinguish between the practitioner's role as part of the key working system and their role in developing a key person relationship with their key children (Manning-Morton and Thorp 2001; Elfer *et al.* 2002).

Important aspects of the key worker system are:

- observing the play of key children and analysing the information gathered through observation;
- planning play experiences for individual children based on observations of their interests;
- sharing information and ideas about play experiences with parents;
- planning play experiences for key group times.

Important aspects of a key person relationship are:

- developing secure trusting relationships with key children and parents through getting to know both child and parents well. This means spending significant amounts of time being and playing with the child.
- developing secure trusting relationships with key children through taking primary responsibility for their physical care. This means feeding and eating with key children, changing and toileting, dressing and washing and settling key children to sleep.
- developing secure trusting relationships with key children through providing a secure base for them. This means supporting their interests and explorations away from the practitioner, perhaps by smiling and nodding as they play and by drawing their attention to interesting things around them, but also being physically and emotionally available to them to come back to, by sitting at their level and in close proximity to them, perhaps on a low chair or bean bag and remaining there rather than moving around the room.

- developing secure trusting relationships with key children through interacting with them using body language, eye contact and voice tone to indicate that the practitioner is available and interested, gauging these according to knowledge of the child's temperament and culture.
- developing secure trusting relationships with key children through understanding children's feelings. This means acknowledging and allowing children to express a range of feelings such as anger, joy, distress, excitement, jealousy and love, and also containing and comforting distressed children by gentle holding, providing words for feelings, offering explanations, empathy and reassurances calmly and gently.

By adopting these practices practitioners can support the children in developing emotional intelligence (Goleman 1996) or literacy (Sharp 2001). Past views of young children's emotional lives have included ideas that have denied the range and complexity of their feelings and have advocated that strong feelings should be repressed. These views are still apparent in some instances today; 'Come on, don't cry, you're a big boy now' or 'Be a nice girl, share your teddy' are phrases that are still heard. Children's expression of pain, distress and anger is particularly uncomfortable for adults, who often respond by frantic jiggling up and down of a baby or distraction of a toddler and then reassuring themselves with the false notion that the child will soon forget their distress.

Implications for practitioners

Just as Shuttleworth (in Miller *et al.* 1989) describes the concept of 'container–contained' as the way in which a mother is able to get in contact with her baby's state of mind, so can practitioners caring for young babies also experience an intense engagement with babies and consequently their own baby-like feelings can be provoked. The more open or receptive the practitioner is to being stirred up emotionally forms the basis for their capacity to be responsive to the children in their care. That is, if they allow themselves to feel and understand their own upset or uncomfortable feelings, then they may then be able to use this understanding to relate to and respond sensitively to those of the baby.

To withstand the emotional impact of a young child's feelings requires practitioners to have a sufficiently strong yet flexible sense of their own adult identity. This includes:

- a high level of self-acceptance;
- an ability to understand how, as adults, we may see ourselves in particular children and them in us;
- an ability to separate out traits and feelings that belong to the adult and not to the child.

By retaining their own sense of adultness, practitioners can remember that they are in benevolent charge of managing their relationship with the child so will not expect babies or toddlers to understand and consider the practitioner's needs or follow the adult's play agenda.

Aspects of individual temperament also affect the adult's ability to cope. A particular baby will provoke a particular set of feelings in an adult. A very bubbly, active adult may find a very placid baby boring or frustrating or a shy adult may find an outgoing child uncomfortably assertive. Understanding that the degree of fit between adult and child will affect their ability to respond and play (Thomas and Chess 1980) means that practitioners need to develop self-awareness in order that they can adapt their responses to each child.

As Shuttleworth also points out, sustaining the impact of someone else's state of mind can be inherently disturbing and emotionally draining (in Miller et al. 1989). Practitioners may then seek ways of avoiding responding to a child. Studies by writers and researchers (such as Hopkins 1988; Goldschmied and Jackson 1994; Elfer 1996; Manning-Morton 2000a), have observed practitioners preferring to busy themselves with impersonal tasks rather than engaging in play with their key children.

This level of emotional demand can lead to practitioners expressing discomfort with the practice of key working. This might be at a personal level such as, 'I don't want to get too close to the children, it's too painful when they leave' or pressures within a team such as, 'It's very difficult in my group, I think I should feed my key baby all the time but my co-worker says I'm spoiling her and she needs to get used to all of us.' Sometimes their discomfort is due to a lack of understanding that encouraging a baby or toddler to develop a close relationship with their key person does not lessen the love between the child and their parents; in fact it broadens the child's experience of responsive trusting relationships.

As Bowlby (1969: 367) says:

> When a child has more than one attachment figure it might well be supposed that his attachment to his principle figure would be weak and conversely that when he has only one figure

his attachment to that one would be specially intense. This, however, is not so: Indeed precisely the opposite is reported.

This highlights that, just as for mothers, the practitioner's capacity for containment is dependent on factors beyond his or her love of children. Emotionally intelligent practice depends on practitioners developing their own emotional literacy and intrapersonal skills (Manning-Morton 2000b). In addition to these, practitioners need sufficient external supports that, in turn, 'contain' the practitioner. They need regular opportunities to reflect on their own emotional responses to the children and to their work, as well as thinking about the children's progress and planning play experiences. For example the practitioners working with Nena found watching the video and talking about their own and Nena's feelings in the situation helpful and illuminating. As Peter Elfer says 'it is difficult to sustain close and responsive relationships with young children without an organisational culture that expects and supports a process of reflection on the emotional dimension of practice' (1996: 30).

This requires that managers, trainers and advisers are themselves sufficiently emotionally literate and knowledgeable about young children's needs to provide support, to value the emotional aspects of practice and to limit unnecessary demands made on the practitioner that would otherwise reduce the amount of physical and mental energy they can make available to the children. Practitioners who are expected to clean, cook and do laundry cannot also play for prolonged periods with the children.

Play experiences for physically and emotionally dependent children from birth to three

In this chapter we have emphasized the importance of the adult/child relationship for this emotionally and physically dependent age group. It is not surprising then, that babies love to play interactive games with people with whom they feel secure. Each time the baby makes eye contact with their close adult carers the response they get gives them a message (positive or negative) about themselves and the world around them.

Imitation games

A great deal of enjoyment and learning comes from the adult holding the baby on their lap and when eye contact has been established, making facial expressions which the baby can imitate. Soon the baby will fill the pause between smiles, tongue poking, eyebrow raising etc. with their attempt to copy. This can continue for as long as eye contact is maintained. The reverse of this game is equally valuable. By imitating the baby's movements or vocalizations the adult is saying I'm interested in you, I enjoy you, I value what you do. Through such play both adult and baby get to know each other better and increase their ability to tune in to each other and to converse. The baby is also learning facial expressions, which they can use later to express their moods.

Disappearing games

The significance of peek-a-boo, which can be played on any occasion with subtle or vigorous movements, should not be underestimated. The adult can disappear behind their hands or close their eyes and reappear with an exaggerated expression of surprise to the delight of the watching baby. Adult or baby can disappear by covering their faces with a cloth or hat. The older baby will want to take control of the game by covering themselves up or snatching the cloth from the adult's face. Toddlers love to initiate this game by hiding their whole

Toddlers love to hide their whole bodies.

bodies behind curtains for example, and their love of repetition means the game can last for a long time. This type of game allows babies and toddlers to play in a safe way with the scary prospect of their carer disappearing and to have some control over how long the separation lasts. Tents, boxes and many other inside/under/behind play experiences also have these benefits.

Shared experiences

Other play experiences that build positive experiences of togetherness are singing, dancing and storytelling. In a 0–3 group these activities differ greatly from the nursery class storytime for 3–5-year-olds. The objective of enabling the babies and toddlers time to sit on laps and enjoy closeness and shared experience is equal to that of developing language skills or understanding rhythm. These times also provide opportunities to make links between home and nursery as favourite books can travel between the two settings. Books or albums containing pictures of individual children's friends, family and pets will enhance their sense of belonging and provide opportunity for feelings to be discussed. For example:

> Jermaine's brother has recently had a birthday and although he enjoyed aspects of the celebrations he struggled with other parts. His mother told his key person about this, so they read *Spot's Birthday Party* together and talked about both the fun of the games and how sad the others felt when only Spot had presents to open.

Feeling secure

Babies' and toddlers' play is much richer and more focused when they do not have to worry that their key person will disappear without telling them. The presence of a child's transitional object can also enable the child to relax and enjoy the play experiences provided. A trailing blanket may not be ideal on a climbing frame but tied safely round the toddler's waist it will accommodate their need for security and support their active play, while also giving the message that their needs are understood, supported and respected. Other children can learn to respect another's special toy; toddlers have been known to return lost or discarded objects to their owners.

Personalized play

The best play experiences are those that the perceptive key person has finely tuned to the interests, concerns and level of ability of their key children. For example:

> Bridie provided disposable cameras in the baby room for Roshan, whose father is a photographer. Carlton introduced cardboard boxes into the home corner when Ethan's family was moving house. Lucy strung different objects from the treasure basket across a corner for Donna who has recently discovered she can deliberately hit things with her waving.

Therapeutic play

Practitioners are generally familiar with the value of water play, paint, sand and clay to enable children to express their feelings. However, the observation above of boxes for the house mover is also a good example of the sort of play experiences that enable even very young children to express their anxieties through play. Ethan was very unclear about what would be left behind. He was worried about his bed not fitting in a box, and why his dad said the toilet was not going with them.

Outdoor play

Non-mobile babies benefit from outdoor play just as much as toddlers. A suitably attired baby can experience the feel of the wind on their skin, the warmth of the sun, watch the movement of the mobile children and see the shadows. The infant can hear the trees rustle and the birds sing, touch the grass, be pulled along in a trolley or enjoy the motion of a swing. However, they are dependent on their carers to be prepared to take them out and to stay close by.

Familiarity and challenge

Good quality play experiences will take account of both the urge to explore and be independent and the tendency to develop sudden fears that is characteristic of this age group. Much of babies' security comes from the predictability of their world. They can be unsettled and upset if their favourite things disappear and new strange things appear in their place, just as we would hate to come home one day and find everything different. Ensuring familiar play resources continue to be available and that novelty and new challenges are introduced slowly and thoughtfully can achieve this.

All the play experiences discussed above are designed to build on the close, supportive relationship between carer and child that will enable them to gradually become strong and independent. They are created to give babies and toddlers positive messages about themselves and the world around them.

3

CHILDREN FROM BIRTH TO THREE PLAYING, GROWING AND LEARNING THROUGH MOVING AND DOING

Learning to move, learning to play

Raj is a 20-month-old boy, one of six babies in a community day nursery baby room. Raj was pushing a cart round the garden on a sunny September day. He was wearing a coat, a hat and a scarf.

'His mum worries about him catching a cold if he plays outdoors as he's had so many chest infections,' His key person Jo, said. 'She wanted him kept inside, but now she's agreed he can play outside and I've promised to wrap him up warmly in whatever she brings in.'

Raj appeared confident and engrossed in his task. His circuit of the garden included navigating the narrow space between the sandpit and the fence, adjusting his cartload of SMA tins from time to time and calling 'Bye bye' to Jo, each time he passed her. It also involved pausing when Jasmine (age 2), the leader of this tour of the garden, halted abruptly shouting 'No go' and then 'Ready, ready go'.

Later, at sleep time Raj took off his own shoes and once Jo had got his socks past his heels, he took his socks off too. Placing them carefully in his basket he quickly found his bed by the bookshelf where it always was, and laid down with 'dog-dog'.

Before he fell asleep Jo could hear him chanting, ' 'Eady, 'eady go' and 'No go' like a mantra. He seemed to be reliving his experiences in the garden that morning. Jo made a note to tell his mum about this.

Physical play is important

Anyone caring for or observing babies and toddlers cannot fail to notice their enthusiasm for physical play, as seen in the example above. Stonehouse (1988) describes this as a characteristic of this age group. They are always on the move, busy and curious, exploring everything they can reach with their whole bodies. Physical play is not only what young children love to do, it is what they need to do in order to gain control of their bodies; to grow in mobility, agility, dexterity and as a result, in independence.

Traditionally, learning about the 'milestones' of young children's physical development has been the overriding focus of the early years practitioner's training. In more recent years the focus has shifted towards children's cognitive development and consequently, reflecting on and planning for children's physical play is now sometimes overlooked. Effective practitioners prioritize refining their knowledge of children's physical development because they understand that physical play is fundamental to all aspects of children's development and learning, including the development of the child's brain.

In the observation of Raj's play above, it can be seen how being able to move around freely and to celebrate what his body can do has a direct impact on all areas of his development.

Communication skills

Communication skills and the desire to communicate are increased if there is something interesting to communicate about and someone interested to communicate with, as anyone who has been housebound or in a monotonous job will agree. During Raj's exacting endeavours in the garden he uses well-known phrases and learns new words in the context of his game, which he later plays with as he falls asleep.

Social development

Social development is promoted as a baby's growing agility and dexterity enables them to play with others. This is a rich source of learning. Now mobile, Raj can join in more – he can follow and imitate older 'experts' in the garden, which is another characteristic of his age (Stonehouse 1989) and he is able to move away from and maintain contact with his key person.

Emotional development

Raj's emotional development, high self-esteem, confidence and independence can be observed as he is enabled to gain control and enjoy what his body can do through physical play and as he prepares to sleep. Not being allowed to play out of doors had been the source of a great deal of frustration, anger and low self-esteem. His mother had not appreciated his need to be active, and his limited social skills and strong feelings (which are further characteristics of this age group), resulted in frequent angry outbursts and tears. Raj's mobility now brings him into contact with new, strange experiences and fear and excitement increase.

Creativity

Creativity develops as a direct result of babies' and toddlers' growing agility and dexterity. Once new tools or materials have been thoroughly investigated to see what they are and what they can do, they are played with imaginatively and incorporated into a game. For example:

> The curtain becomes the means for a peep-bo game; a paint-brush swiped from side to side in a horizontal trajectory becomes the action of a fast car, often accompanied by sound effects. In the observation of Raj, we also see Jasmine who is now a competent tricycle rider and uses her physical skill to support her creation of a 'bus stop' game in which she practices her leadership skills.

Learning to move

Those caring for children from birth to three will be familiar with the general sequence of physical development and its relation to play in the first three years. Effective practitioners will also have a good understanding of the impact of wider social, cultural and historical trends as well as the immediate environment on young children's development and therefore the uniqueness of each child's individual physical development.

After nine months curled up in the womb a baby's stretching, vigorous random kicking and arm waving helps the baby uncurl (Karmiloff-Smith 1994). This activity strengthens those early weak muscle fibres and at the same time changes are taking place in the baby's brain. Involuntary actions (subcortex controlled) are being

*Babies and toddlers celebrate what their bodies
can do in their enthusiasm for physical play.*

taken over by intentional voluntary actions (controlled by the
cerebral cortex). Increasingly specialized structures are being laid
down which will lead to even greater muscle control.

Gaining head and neck control

This requires considerable strength, as at birth the baby's head is
disproportionately large compared to an adult's. A baby's head
flops if not supported, which is great if you need to fit into a very
confined space like the womb (Karmiloff-Smith 1994), however
it's not so helpful if you want to have a good look round!

> Omar (9 weeks) is laid on his stomach; he strives to hold up his
> shoulders as well as his head so that he can see and better hear
> his key person who is sitting on the settee feeding and chatting

to another baby. She pauses to chat to Omar as they make eye contact.

Now he is able to see more of the world he is motivated to gain further control so he can explore these sights and sounds and integrate them into his play with movement and sound.

Rolling over

As babies vigorously kick and wave their arms and legs and lift their heads they may accidentally discover rolling over. The accidental rolling soon becomes intentional rolling play for the enjoyment of the experience.

> Hannah's key person said that Hannah (7 months) plays at rolling over at every opportunity. She rolls towards the objects she cannot reach, she tries to roll over when being changed, and has rolled off the settee at home two or three times.

(At this age babies do not learn about the danger of drops from experience.)

Sitting up

Sitting up is usually achieved between 5 and 9 months, although different childcare practices will affect when this happens. At first babies may only have sufficient balance to sit briefly; after having been pulled up into this position they may start to topple over as the neuromuscular control which moves from head downwards and from the centre of the baby's body outwards is only halfway there, hence the sag at the waist (Karmiloff-Smith 1994).

As both back muscles and balance improve the baby will sit confidently, spread-legged for balance. Being able to sit up opens up new opportunities for play. Now for the first time the baby is upright and is ideally positioned to reach for and explore objects with their hands. Sarah, as shown in the case study in Chapter 6, was able to explore a wealth of materials now that she was able to sit and play with the contents of her Treasure Basket (Goldschmied and Jackson 1994). This position also brought her into face-to-face contact with Gemma and Milo, the sitting babies in her baby room. The objects they explored together often acted as a catalyst for communication between them (Goldschmied and Selleck 1996).

Much as lying babies discover rolling over, sitting babies may fall forward and lift themselves up on their arms. They may notice that they can move themselves around in a circle or that vigorous swimming like movements will propel them forward when they are lying on their front. These movements may become crawling, even though that may be backwards at first due to their disproportionately heavy head (Karmiloff-Smith 1994).

Crawling

Crawling is a complex action to learn; the baby has to plan how and when to move each arm and leg in order to get to where they are aiming. They do not have adult models to imitate, and many end up moving in very different ways. Some babies miss this activity out completely, preferring to pull themselves straight up onto their feet.

Whether a baby crawls conventionally or not is not important; the variations are evidence of the babies' active role in making sense of their actions and learning how to use them effectively.

> Morwenna moves to satisfy her great desire to have control over her body so she can better explore and increase her control over her environment through her play. She has decided she wants to reach the train set her sister is playing with. She recognizes the sound of its motor and knows exactly where to find it – in her sister's bedroom.

The route to this forbidden territory is one of the mental maps she has formed since becoming mobile; this has also enabled her to practice cognitive skills such as memory and intentionality (Gopnik *et al.* 1999).

At around 7 to 9 months old babies' experience of fear greatly increases:

> Kofi (8 months) cries when a visiting aunty tries to pick him up. His mother says that a few weeks ago everyone was greeted with a smile. Now he is only happy to be left with those he knows well.

It is perhaps not surprising that this coincides with the new freedom babies have gained to go off independently as they play. This new surge of fear does have some positive effects. Being able to crawl means babies are able to get into more dangerous situations than before; however, most mature crawlers seem to have a fear of danger not previously evident (Gibson and Walk 1960).

Wayne (9 months) crawled to the top step of the patio and cried for his key person to come and get him.

However, this is not true for all babies:

Lucy (10 months) crawled off the step from the dining room to the kitchen to reach mum and fell face down on the kitchen floor.

Depth perception is now believed to be present at birth; however, there is much debate whether a sense of danger comes with maturation of visual perception or with experience of locomotion (Karmiloff-Smith 1994).

Rader *et al.* (1980) found babies experienced in using a baby walker were as reluctant to crawl across the 'deep' side of the visual cliff as babies who had only got about by crawling. However, they also found that the babies with baby walker experience did cross if in the baby walkers. Rader concluded that visual clues are disrupted when babies move about in artificial devices. Perhaps the crawlers, who could use tactile clues as well as visual ones, were able to be more sensitive to depth and therefore were more cautious. Other experiments found this was not the case; however the much publicized dangers of baby walkers means that adults should err on the side of caution and avoid the use of walkers whatever the outcome of this particular debate.

Practice at crawling increases muscular strength in the baby's arms and legs.

Wayne uses everything in reach to pull himself up. However, he cannot yet get down. His key person reported that the challenge she currently has is to ensure everything in reach will bear his weight and to be on hand to rescue him when he wants to get down.

A baby soon discovers they can cruise around the furniture until a gap appears that is too large to cross.

Lucy leans towards the next piece of furniture with her hands outstretched but does not move her feet. She falls forward, then if not too shaken, crawls across the gap.

Both Wayne's and Lucys upright position and higher eye level and arm reach affects their play. It means they are experts at clearing low tables and shelves. However, the negative implications for play are that when they are cruising they do not have their hands free for exploration and carrying.

Walking

This commences with a few wobbly steps. The baby is encouraged to persist at refining this new skill by their caregivers' joyous response to this achievement. However walking really slows the baby down at first, so when in a hurry they may still resort to crawling. The baby may also resort to crawling for managing slopes or stairs. They are not just learning to walk but to become mobile, and that means being able to adapt their method of locomotion to particular circumstances.

> Jamie (12 months) waddles from side to side as he walks, without bending his knees. Books and the remote control for the TV all get trodden on. He steps on a wax crayon that rolls under his foot and down he goes.

Gradually the splayed feet and stiff legged gait of new walkers improves and they become able to go round objects instead of trampling over them. They can stop, go backwards and soon can run (Karmiloff-Smith 1994); these movements soon become central features of their play.

It is important to remember that walking is just another means of exploring and playing for toddlers. They seem to want to celebrate their newly gained level of mobility in their play. Stonehouse (1988) likens this to a teenager who has just learnt to drive. They may be so attracted to the exciting things they encounter that they cannot resist the temptation to go and explore them.

> Johan's mother reported, 'When going to the shop he seems to have a completely different agenda from me. He often toddles off in the opposite direction or stops, waits, and then sets off again for no apparent reason. When we get to steps he wants to go up and down them three or four times before moving on.'

Many toddlers enjoy the challenge of playing on steps. At first going up stairs involves using one foot to stabilize weight and the other turned out as a lever. Thus they need both feet to arrive on each step before moving on to the next one (Karmiloff-Smith 1994). This is also the case going down. Adults can teach toddlers to go down in a backward crawl for safety.

Gradually between 24 and 30 months further physical changes take place. Legs lengthen, fat is converted into muscle and the baby appears less chubby; they become much more upright, arches develop in the toddler's feet, making them less flat footed, and knees and ankles have greater flexibility (Karmiloff-Smith 1994).

Physical play now includes such composite skills as being able to climb a ladder to reach the top of a slide, steer and scoot themselves along on a tricycle and (as seen in the observation of Raj) steer trucks and prams, loaded with their collections around a complex circuit.

Three-year-olds reach their level of mobility, agility, dexterity and independence through the interplay of three things: the maturation of the nervous system and muscle fibres, the child's insatiable appetite to explore and control their own body and their environment; and the physical play experiences and opportunities they are able to engage in that motivate and support them.

Holding, manipulating and doing

A newborn baby's ability to build on their existing grasp reflex through waving, reaching and gradually refining their grasp is the basis upon which their creative use of tools for both expression and survival is built (Karmiloff-Smith 1994). As babies play with these

Feedback from the effect of play perfects skills in measuring distance and force.

gestures, muscular strength develops down through the arm eventually to reach the fingertips and they gradually increase their control over their movements. Feedback from the effect of this play encourages practice, bringing the neural pathways for perception and action into synchrony and perfecting skills in measuring distance and force (Gopnik *et al.* 1999).

Claudia (3 months) lying on her back, accidentally batted some metal measuring spoons strung across her cot. The clatter and swinging of the spoons attracted her attention and motivated Claudia to try again and again to recreate this effect.

When a baby can grasp objects they play with them by exploring them with their mouths to find out more about them. Karmiloff-Smith (1994) states that the mouth, tongue and lips are the first areas to develop in the cerebral cortex. This is the part that controls voluntary action and there are twice as many nerve endings in the mouth as in the fingertips, giving feedback about shape, texture and size. Sarah, in Chapter 6, can be seen turning this information into a visual reconstruction, allowing her to recognize an object she has had in her mouth but never seen before (Gopnik *et al.* 1999).

Gradually the ability to grasp is refined and a baby can also let go. Noah has perfected this art.

Noah is sitting in his cot. He usually has a large collection of stuffed toys in there with him. He calls to his key person, David. David enters the sleep area, and finds that Noah has pushed every toy small enough through the bars on to the floor. He has also taken off and cast his socks out of the cot and his dummy. David goes to take Noah out of the cot but Noah protests. To Noah's delight David understands what is required and retrieves everything so Noah can begin the game again.

This game reinforces pathways in Noah's brain that control planning and prediction and the ability to remember objects after they have disappeared (object permanence) (Gopnik *et al.* 1999).

Developing a pincer grasp (usually between 8 and 12 months) is as important as the first step and first word, yet does not usually attract the same kind of attention. This action, combined with the later development of a rotating wrist and hand and eye coordination can be seen in Una's play:

Una (2½ years) was sticking. In one hand she held a box of small pieces of coloured paper that she had torn up, holding it against her body for extra support. She was using the other hand to take out the pieces of paper one by one, between her finger and thumb and place them on the surface of a sheet of very sticky paper. She had previously smothered this with layers of glue using a spatula.

She now has the necessary skills to use a whole range of tools to support her growing independence; these enhance her play and enable her to enter into the cultural world of using symbols.

Perceiving understanding and learning

Babies' learning is founded on their sensory play experiences. Through the experiences that the baby and toddler perceive through their senses, synaptic connections are made in the developing brain. Annette Karmiloff-Smith describes this as a fundamental idea to understanding children's development; that it 'is a constant interaction between the emerging structures of the brain and the baby's experience of the world' (1994: 26).

Rita Carter (1999) describes how this process is interactive in the act of perception; that an initial perceptive experience will alter

Sensory play is a prime source of learning.

the structure of the brain, which will in turn influence how an object is perceived and so on, thereby building a more complex synaptic network. The implication of this for practitioners is that the more varied and appropriate the play experience offered to the child, the better the essential connections between the neural cells will be.

> Jeanette, after learning about children's perceptual development, now planned sensory play experiences for the babies. In the non-mobile baby area she displayed faces and black and white geometric pattern pictures around the bottom of the walls. She strung a variety of objects across their rug, such as keys, rice in a small sealed cardboard box and bells. The texture, weight and temperature of the loofah made a good contrast with the metal spoon. The lemon she gave to one baby to hold offered him an interesting smell.

Sighted adults tend to over rely on their sense of sight to give them information about the world, but for a new baby vision is the least well-developed part of the sensory system. However, babies' tracking reflexes and attraction to moving objects stimulate the visual areas of the brain and when the retinas merge, they can see more clearly where things are and what they are. Now they can study detailed features of faces, not just outlines and can remember faces too.

Perceptual development does not happen in discrete areas but cross-modally. The baby's interactions with their carer brings together the way their carer looks, smells, sounds and moves.

Sound, taste and smell are often overlooked when practitioners consider sensory play experiences but a baby's hearing is as good as an adult's at birth and sound and smell are key ways in which a baby distinguishes between people they know and those they do not.

> Jeanette also used her new understanding to help settle new babies. She asked parents to teach her how they rocked, comforted and got their babies to sleep. She asked for them to bring cot bedding from home smelling of their detergent, and even laid one of the mum's worn T-shirts over her when feeding a new, unsettled baby.

Babies recognize familiar touch and movement, their sense of proprioception tells them where their limbs are without looking.

These abilities to recognize and recall features of people and objects through sensory information shows the fundamental cognitive process of memory at work early in an infant's life. Being able to draw on a perceptual memory helps young children to recall events, as we saw in the observation of Billie in Chapter 2. Six-month-old babies can form event memories that can be retrieved two years later in the presence of the right reminders. This was shown by children of 2½ years returning to a laboratory where they had played a game at the age of 6 months. Although these children were no more likely than other children to pick out the toy previously used in the game, they were more likely to repeat the required reaching play to find the toy unprompted, especially if they heard the sound of the rattle used in the original game (Perris *et al.* 1990).

Many adults are familiar with the startling clarity of a memory prompted by a smell or sound; such an experience reflects the close connection between these areas of the brain.

> Lydia as a baby of 2 months could often be soothed when crying by singing to her. Her mother was a singer and pianist and music was an integral part of her experience at home.

Our growing knowledge of the important links between mobility, dexterity, perception and brain development seem to support Piaget's view that sensory-motor experiences and abilities are a primary source of information for children like Raj, whose active exploration of the garden has an important role in his acquisition of knowledge.

This means that the core of learning for children like Una, Noah, Raj and Tommy is active, hands-on play experience. This allows them to create images in their minds that have meaning, which form a firm basis for thinking and support for developing abstract ideas and symbolic representation of language, numbers or letters.

Changing perceptions of physical play

Play as surplus energy

Children's physical play has not always been seen as valuable. At the end of the nineteenth century, Spencer saw play merely as a means of letting off surplus energy. His view was that the energy formerly used for hunting or fighting was expended in play, as these original demands no longer exist (Spencer 1878, cited in Smith *et al.* 1998: 192). It is true that young children can seem to be bursting with energy and needing to let off steam, especially newly mobile toddlers. However, this provides us with a narrow view of physical play, which may impact negatively on our practice.

Practitioners working with children from birth to three who sub-scribe to this surplus energy theory may take toddlers in the garden for short periods of vigorous play so that they will be able to come in and sit down to concentrate on the 'valuable' indoor activities afterwards. Babies may only be taken out in buggies. There will be less planning and resources for outdoor play and a lack of provision for babies' and toddlers' physical play indoors. Yet, not to provide opportunities and support for physical play works against the inter-ests of babies and toddlers and undermines their efforts to explore their world.

Piaget and sensory-motor play

Play with motion is one of the first types of play that adults engage in with babies. They bounce them on their knees and clap their hands together, developing patterns of play such as in pat-a-cake. As with social games such as peek-a-boo, babies are active in instigating, prolonging or stopping physical games through using their gaze or vocalizations. Babies also play with motion on their own, wriggling and kicking for the pure enjoyment of the effect of their movements.

Piaget (1962) sees babies engaging in play from as early as the second stage of the sensory-motor period, at about 2 months old. He perceives the children as dynamic organisms striving to make sense of their environment and in the process of doing this creating mental structures or schemas. For Piaget cognitive change happens through the mechanisms of assimilation, whereby the world is interpreted through existing schemas, and accommodation whereby an existing schema is changed to take account of new experiences. As the process of accommodation involves the child in trying to comprehend the experience, play only occurs as the assimilated experience is repeated in practice. Babies and toddlers can often be observed struggling seriously with the physical exploration of a movement but thereafter repeating it gleefully; Piaget called this mastery play (1962).

The authors have seen this kind of play to be supported effectively in good quality provision for babies and toddlers every day. Although Piaget's theory has been criticized and found wanting in some respects, there is no theory that has been so supportive to practice in this respect because it is the most overarching so far in relation to motor play. Piaget's work has had a very strong influence on the way the early years curriculum is presented, as he believed that children learn through play by being free to act on their environment (1962), the key role for the practitioner in this approach is to create a stimulating environment for the babies and toddlers to explore. This is an essential part of a curriculum for children from birth to three. However, if the concept of the adult as an important component of that environment is not fully understood, practitioners may develop a very 'hands off' approach to play, when many play situations require practitioners to adopt the role of play partner or facilitator as well as provider and observer.

The links between physical play, development and learning

Molly Davies describes children as having 'a natural appetite for movement, an appetite which requires as much consideration and attention as their appetite for food, drink, rest and sleep' (1995/ 2002: 41). Satisfying young children's appetite for food and drink enables them to grow in size, weight, strength and height. Satisfying children's appetite for movement through the provision of opportunities for physical play facilitates children's physical development, which Maude (2001: 6) defines as, 'the process through which children gain co-ordination, movement skills and abilities and become physically literate'. This, in turn, has a direct impact on all other areas of development and play. It also has a significant impact on a child's self-concept, as could be seen from the change in Raj once

Rich opportunities for physical play have an impact on all areas of development.

he was able to practise and refine his agility and dexterity. The importance of providing children from birth to three with rich opportunities for physical play that are finely tuned to the characteristics of this age group and to each individual child cannot be overemphasized. This can be compared to adults who experience a huge psychological benefit from perfecting physical skills and becoming fitter. They describe themselves as able to think more clearly, feel more confident at work and to have pride in their bodies.

Literacy may not be uppermost in the minds of those providing physical play experiences for children from birth to three. However, a correlation has been found between balance, fine motor skills and reading ability. It has been discovered that children with learning difficulties and those who are dyslexic often had poor hand–eye coordination and balance. An exercise programme that mimics the physical movements of early infancy, such as babies stretching their limbs when lying on their backs and crawling, was found to produce a significant improvement in children's literacy (Goddard 2002). It may be that children also experience some of the positive psychological effects described previously, which in turn motivates them to persist in a task that they do not find easy. If a link does exist, the significance of providing play experiences that motivate babies and toddlers to fully use their physical skills is further strengthened.

The role of the adult in physical play

Safety and danger, confidence and fear

If practitioners refer back to the hugely significant role of the key person in relation to young children's physical and emotional dependency, they will recognize the importance of the key person relationship in supporting physical development and play. This is particularly pertinent in relation to supporting children's confidence in their physical explorations. It is important that practitioners are alert to possible danger but do not allow unnecessary restrictions or their own fears to overly reduce children's physical adventures. A baby or toddler will refer back to their close adult when exploring away from them and will pick up the adult's anxiety and may learn that it is only safe to play near to the adult. Adults tend to give this message more to girls than to boys (Whyte 1983).

> Kate (12 months) crawled through the door out towards the climbing frame. Her key person watched as she started up the ramp. This was the third time this week that she had attempted

this. As she reached the top, her key person moved the soft mats closer to the apparatus and stood nearby. Kate stood up, balancing herself with one hand, then she let go, making excited sounds and smiling; she waved and moved one leg closer to the edge of the platform. Then she fell backwards onto her bottom. She looked up at her key person who held out her hand, smiled and helped her to slide down.

Kate clearly has the necessary attentive support of her key person as she sets herself this physical challenge. The key person is balancing her desire to protect Kate with the need to allow her to explore. By striking this balance she is able to provide a secure base for Kate during this daring adventure.

Safety is (rightly) always uppermost in practitioner's minds but an environment that is too safe will lack challenge. Children may become bored and fractious with each other or find challenges that practitioners will find less acceptable, for example, trying to escape from the room or climbing on tables.

Teamwork

Practitioners who have a supportive relationship and who respect each other will find it easier to manage the conflicting demands of providing a secure base for key children and the need to keep an overview of a play environment that offers challenge to curious, explorative children. An example of how this can be arranged to benefit the children is as follows.

In discussion with colleagues it was decided that they would take it in turn to act as manager each morning and afternoon. The manager would deal with the phone, tissues, etc. and re-ordering the environment when too many things had been 'transported'. Then the other two could concentrate on playing with the toddlers.

(Manning-Morton and Thorp 2001)

Observing and reflecting

Practitioners who know their key children well, who spend time observing and reflecting on the play they see, will be able to plan new challenges and sensitively offer more resources to extend well practised skills. This will also enable them to judge when to offer help, to not presume that help is required, and only to help enough to facilitate more independence for the baby or toddler. They will also be sensitive to children's preferences in relation to physical handling in such tasks as nose wiping, or being cuddled, carried, holding hands or rough and tumble play. This means being tuned in to children's signals and alert to their own feelings of rejection, which may spill over into inappropriate comments when a child avoids their hug such as, 'Oh, don't you love me any more? I'm going to cry now.' Practitioners who respect children's right to begin, stop or reject physical interactions are providing a good model of physical interactions between people (Manning-Morton and Thorp 2001).

Partnership between parents and practitioners

Practitioners must understand the cultural differences between families in relation to physical expression of affection. It is important that parents and practitioners know each others' expectations and each others' fears for their baby or toddler in relation to physical play. Mixed messages will confuse the child and undermine their confidence.

> Gina (20 months) is always spoonfed by her mum at home, while her key person Anila sees Gina as one of the oldest children and encourages her to feed herself. Gina's attempts are messy but effective.

Gina can cope with the two approaches continuing provided the parent and key person have discussed this. The difficulty comes when Gina is told 'That's dirty' if she feeds herself at home yet, when she waits to be fed at nursery, she is waiting a long time and is thought of as lazy or lacking fine motor skills.

By looking back at the observation of Raj a good example can be seen of how a parent, anxious about their child's health, has been listened to and respected. A compromise has been reached and consequentially Raj directly benefits from the trusting relationship that has built up between his mother and key person.

Play experiences for active children from birth to three

Because of the significance of physical development on every other area of development, including brain development, the challenge to practitioners working with this age group is to provide the sort of physical play experiences that will support and promote physical development.

Maude suggests physical play opportunities should provide the following opportunities for children (2001: 29):

- to develop motor, rhythmic and kinaesthetic sense;
- to develop dexterity and skill in manipulating objects;
- to develop hand and eye coordination;
- to develop body and spatial awareness, as well as awareness of physical capabilities and limitations.

This checklist could be used as a guide when setting up or evaluating the choice of play experiences available for a group of children aged from birth to three.

Opportunities for constant practice

If babies' and toddlers' physical skills are to be refined and perfected they need practice and lots of it. Moreover, the enjoyment of repetition is a key characteristic of young children. Adults thinking about physical skills they have striven to achieve – for example, learning to drive – will recall that what really helped was having many opportunities to practise, and trying to use the skills gained in different circumstances. In a nursery setting, this means having a range of resources to support physical play available most of the time. Settings that provide these play opportunities for most of the day indoors and outside will have agile children, confident in what their bodies can do.

Similarly, fine motor skills such as pouring or drawing cannot be refined without constant repetition. Workshop areas that always have the basic tools and materials available are ideal. Moreover, if additions are introduced to provide the opportunity for young children to use that skill in a different or more complex way then children will become more accomplished and interest will be sustained. The resulting rise in confidence will provide motivation to go even further. Keeping the basic resources available alongside new materials also allows the child to return to simpler tasks when feeling less like a challenge and caters for the range of abilities in the group.

To refine physical skills babies and toddlers need practice and lots of it.

Physical activities babies and toddlers enjoy

Everyone learns more and is more likely to engage in a subject or activity if they are interested in it and enjoy doing it. Those caring for children from birth to three will be able to recall many occasions when a baby or toddler has given a new expensive toy a swift glance and then proceeded to spend 20 minutes of focused play exploring the box. If practitioners were to draw up a checklist of physical play that babies and toddlers enjoy, the list would probably contain many of the activities shown in Table 3.1.

This list is not exhaustive, but children able to play in these ways indoors as well as outside, will be developing large and small motor skills and also perceptual and cognitive skills. Young children engaged

Table 3.1 A checklist of physical play that babies and toddlers enjoy

Mouthing, banging, swiping, tipping and filling
Collecting, transporting, lining up objects, wrapping up things or themselves
Pushing, pulling, throwing, putting things or themselves inside, under, on
   top or behind objects and hiding themselves and other objects
Being swung high up, sliding down, balancing, spinning, following, dancing,
   running and rolling.

in these activities will be learning about object permanence, capacity, position, weight, resistance, gravity, and much more.

Resources to facilitate physical play

Children of different abilities can enjoy the resources shown in Table 3.2 at different levels. They offer open-ended experiences, which enable children to explore many different schemas and to be creative and imaginative. Collections of pieces of material, empty containers and many of the resources found in Heuristic Play (Goldschmied and Jackson 1994) can be made available alongside the ones in Table 3.2 so there are resources to transport, wrap, line up, collect and distribute.

The children's interests, their ability to use the materials safely and the adult support available will determine the choice of resources. For example, large smooth pebbles in a Treasure Basket (Goldschmied and Jackson 1994) are safe for sitting babies who have yet to develop the skill of throwing, especially as an adult will be sitting nearby. However, an older toddler who is an enthusiastic thrower, keen to practice it at every opportunity would need very close supervision exploring this particular object. Throwing is great fun and a skill to be encouraged. Toddlers just need help with what to throw and where.

As Darren (19 months) loved throwing, his key person provided a special throwing collection. It included woollen pom-poms, screwed up paper balls, and sponges. If Darren was spotted about to throw a block or anything else unsuitable, the practitioners would say, 'No thank you, Darren. Where's Darren's special throwing things?' In addition, lots of throwing experiences with balls, beanbags and targets were set up in the garden.

Table 3.2 Resources to facilitate physical play

Hollow cubes
A cupboard under a work surface with a curtain across instead of a door
Small slides and climbing frames
Tents, tunnels, very large cardboard boxes
Carts, buggies, tricycles
A pile of cushions covered by a counterpane for a challenging crawling
    experience
Large empty boxes and tubs some with string attached so they can be pulled
    along
A wooden bar in front of a low mirror for pulling up on

Toddlers soon learn through adults supplying simple rules and safe alternatives.

Pretend play resources

Real resources for pretend play in the home corner provide excellent opportunities to refine and practice large and small motor skills. The younger the child the less advanced fine finger movements will be so the resources shown in Table 3.3 will make a much more toddler-friendly home corner.

Rough and tumble play

Children need to experience being held and rocked but also the excitement of rough and tumble play. Babies enjoy exciting movement if they are in what they perceive to be safe hands. Practitioners can provide these experiences by lifting babies into the air and swinging them slowly down, rocking them and bouncing them on their knees. Chasing and catching games, toddlers launching themselves off walls into their carers arms, and carers' and young children dancing and spinning round together all offer safe but rich kinetic experiences. These games often have rhythms that even very young children recognize and begin to anticipate. Davies (1995/2002: 28) gives this example

> Someone makes a movement starting some way away from the baby which, as it gets nearer and nearer gathers speed and force and culminates in a moment of impact and excitement as the baby is picked up.

Naturally care must be taken regarding location and timing. This is not a good activity just before babies and toddlers will be expected to be calm. Practitioners' physical well-being must also be considered. There must be sufficient space and anticipation of the moment when pleasure is turning into overexcitement and tears.

Table 3.3 Pretend play resources

Real saucepans, colanders, measuring jugs, teapots, changing mats, first size nappies, beds that they can get into, cut-down real brooms and mops, chubby wooden spoons, real plastic picnic sets, hats, bags, waistcoats, shawls, wellington boots and slippers

---

Moving with music

The kind of games described above also reflect the link between babies' and toddlers' understanding of physical rhythm (Trevarthan and Malloch 2002). Young children readily learn the actions accompanying songs and are able to move rhythmically to music long before they are able to sing. Confident practitioners can create opportunities for babies and toddlers to move their bodies and to beat rhythms, to sing and move, throughout the day. The *Key Times* video (Manning-Morton and Thorp 2001) shows Victoria extending one toddler's interest in beating on a slide with his hands to beating rhythms all over the garden. Each surface – trees, barrels, walls and up-turned tins provided a different sound for them to play their tune on.

Group action song times that are only used to fill gaps between tidying up and lunch communicate that this is an activity adults do not value. Music and song sessions are valuable both at spontaneous times and specifically planned sessions. Babies and toddlers have fun imitating the practitioner and each other; they learn about rhythm and rhyme. They become skilled at representing animals, activities and emotions through actions and expressions. Through simple non-competitive singing and chanting games they learn turn taking and cooperation, for example, 'Isn't It Funny How Bears Like Honey' and 'Ring a Ring a Roses'.

Above all it is important to balance these organized physical play times with lots of opportunity for free flow physical play indoors and outside. This should not be interrupted by too many tidy-up times or care routines. Good quality free flow physical play is initiated by the baby or toddler and supported and extended by the resources and presence of the practitioner.

4

CHILDREN FROM BIRTH TO THREE PLAYING, GROWING AND LEARNING ABOUT THEMSELVES AND OTHERS

Understanding the context for social play

At the lunch table Paulette and Jack (2½ years) are sitting with their key person, Sue, and two other children. Paulette stands up to brush some spilled rice from her chair, Jack points at her, looking at Sue, who explains what Paulette is doing. As she sits down, Jack brushes Paulette's leg with his hand and laughs. 'He holding my feet,' chuckles Paulette.

'Is he tickling your feet?' echoes Sue in surprise. They giggle and Jack does it again, he nearly topples off his chair and they laugh again. Jack slaps his hand downwards, which catches Paulette's hand. 'Ooh careful,' says Sue gently. Jack tickles Paulette again, They giggle.

'Funny, funny, funny,' says another child.

'Are you tickling Paulette?' says Sue in mock horror. He does it again and Paulette turns around in her chair away from him, laughing. 'What's he doing to you?' Sue asks Paulette.

'He ticklin' me.'

'Is he tickling your leg? Are you tickling Paulette's leg, Jack?' Sue smiles at them both.

While another child serves dessert, the game continues on and off. Jack goes and returns from the toilet, and tickles Paulette again. She utters a disgruntled sound and turns her face away as she eats her pudding. After a while Jack does it again and Paulette does not respond. Sue notices and watches her response, Paulette looks at her. 'He ticklin' my leg,' she complains.

'Say to Jack, stop, Jack, no more,' Sue advises.

'Stop, Jack,' and Paulette puts her hand on his arm.

'No more tickling,' says Sue, and Paulette nods her head at him. They carry on eating and talking with another child about his little sister.

(Key Times Video 2001)

Social beings

In contrast to the traditional view of babies and toddlers that sees them as having difficulty in de-centring or seeing things from another's perspective (Piaget 1969) and as only playing alone (Parten 1932), the more recent research of Dunn and Kendrick (1982) has drawn a picture of the empathic, relational child whose social competence is enhanced through their play with others.

Trevarthan points out that the view of the child as an egocentric individual 'a biological and mental isolate' (1995: 98) results in a view of children's socialization as a training of individuals forced to change in order to live with other people. In contrast he puts forward a view of the infant as an 'innate companion and co-operator' (Trevarthan 1995: 98) who is born ready to learn through sharing other people's thoughts and feelings. In this view the communication of emotion has a positive role in the cognitive and social growth of children as

Children's social competence is enhanced through their play with others.

they and their caring adults and peers adjust to one another's states of mind.

In the observation above, Paulette and Jack are clearly experiencing the same, then different emotions to each other at different points in their tickling game. The sensitive support of their feelings by their key person helps them to understand each other better through the medium of their play. In Chapter 2 we looked at the emotional learning that takes place in a baby's first relationships. This is the learning that forms the basis of the child's sense of self and their ability to relate well to others. Children who feel secure in the loving and consistent responses of their parent or key person feel confident as they play in the wider social world. In the observation above we can see how Paulette and Jack feel confident in their key person's positive response to their social play.

So in the process of playing young children learn about themselves and about other people. They find out about their own feelings, thoughts and desires and the feelings, thoughts and desires of others. As they develop their sense of themselves as a separate person they form their self-concept, as reflected back to them in their close relationships. How they come to see themselves as people will affect how they relate to others, their attitudes to new experiences, their dispositions to learning and how they play.

Understanding self

When babies are first born, they largely see themselves as part of their mother and their mother as part of them. They do not recognize their own reflection for many months, but newborn babies are able to imitate adults poking out their tongues. This means they can translate what they see into an action, which shows that at an unconscious level they already have the beginnings of a sense of self (Gopnik *et al.* 1999).

At about 9 months old babies begin to show an interest in their reflections in a mirror and enjoy playing with them. However this interest does not mean that they recognize themselves; it is not until six to nine months later that a child will touch their own face when looking in a mirror rather than reaching out to the reflection. They love to see themselves in pictures and videos at this time and often use their own names when referring to themselves (Smith *et al.* 1998).

Justin (14 months) is involved in an Heuristic Play session (Goldschmied 1994). He sits down with a tin between his legs,

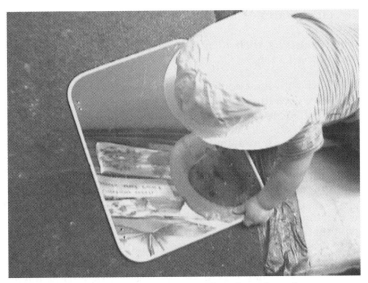

How children come to see themselves affects how they play.

turns the tin over and bangs it with his hands. Justin smiles and as he does so, catches sight of his reflection in the low mirror. He continues to bang the tin, watching himself in the mirror. He crawls over to the mirror and bangs his reflection saying 'Ustin'. He smiles, continuing to bang his hand on the mirror.

This fascination with who they are and how their outer appearance relates to their inner feelings extends into all aspects of a child's self-concept and is manifest in their play. The rapid acquisition of physical skills puts a toddler's body at the centre of their experience. They like to explore themselves, showing great enjoyment of everything their body can do and interest in what it produces. This may include playing with the mucus from their noses or the contents of their nappy. The extent to which a toddler retains a sense of pride and pleasure in their physical self depends largely on the parent's or practitioner's accepting response to their natural curiosity about themselves and others. In the observation at the beginning of the chapter, Sue shows her acceptance of Paulette and Jack's game by her facial expression and reflective commentary but she is also teaching the children about respecting each other's physical privacy.

Children's awareness of their gender, race and ableness

Children construct their identity and attitudes through the inter-action of three factors:

- experience with their bodies;
- experience with their social environments;
- their cognitive developmental stage.

Gender and racial awareness is seen to begin in early toddlerhood when children make observations of their own and other children's bodies. Children can apply gender labels at around 2 years of age and are learning colour names, which they begin to apply to skin colour. They also start to notice physical differences and differences between types of families (Derman-Sparks 1989).

Two-year-olds may be aware of who is a girl or a boy but non-stereotypical cues such as hairstyles or clothing can confuse them. They often show that they think they can be both male and female; for example, boys may play at being pregnant or girls at having a penis. This kind of play provides children with a safe way of coming to terms gradually with the features and limitations of their own biology. In integrated settings, children will also learn about their own and other's abilities and disabilities. For example:

> Billie (2½) and Meg (2½) developed a close friendship. Despite Meg being unable to speak due to her cerebral palsy they com-municated and played together a lot, enjoying each other's company. Billie's mum also reported that Billie liked to play at 'being Meg', which meant having to be carried or using a piece of hardboard as a standing frame when she was playing at home. Her key person agreed with Billie's mum that far from meaning that she was deriding Meg's condition or regressing in her own development, rather that Billie was learning important things in her play about what it is like to have a disability.

So in contrast to the usual notion that they are 'too young to notice', this age is crucial in the formation of children's own identity and their acceptance of diversity.

The impact of bias and oppression

Not only are toddlers noticing differences but they are also differen-tiating between these cues and classifying them by constructing evaluative categories. Identity development then, goes hand in hand with attitude development. At this stage, around 3 years of age, stereotyping and bias will influence children's self-concept and their attitudes towards differences between people and they may exhibit 'pre-prejudice' towards others in their play on the basis of gender, race or being differently abled (Derman-Sparks 1989). These may be less noticeable behaviours such as not wanting to sit next to a black child, hold hands with a disabled child or refusing to let a girl play on a bike.

All young children are harmed by the impact of bias and oppression on their development. Ablism (ascribing a higher value to able-bodied people than to people with disabilities) closes off both play opportunities and the establishment of a proud self-concept for disabled children and it gives a false sense of superiority to able-bodied children.

Gender stereotyping closes off whole areas of play experience to children just because of their sex. Rubin *et al.* (1974) suggest that within the first 24 hours of their baby's life, parents/carers have different expectations of boy babies and girl babies and the games that they play with babies differ. For example, girls are talked to and smiled at more often than boys, an early encouragement of their social skills. Boy babies are held up in the air more frequently while girls are held close to the body. Boys are exposed to much rougher

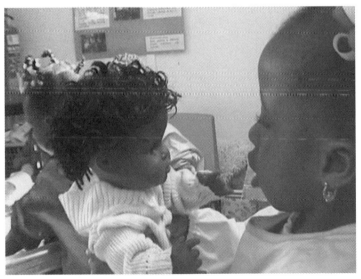

This age is crucial in the formation of children's own identity and their acceptance of diversity.

game playing than girls and are allowed to take more risks (Smith and Lloyd 1978). Many of the toys which are given to babies and young children bring with them a message of 'femininity' or 'masculinity' – think about images where ducks are dressed in dresses or aprons and bears in trousers.

Just as it has been argued that gender differences are understood from a very young age, Siraj-Blatchford (1994) makes a similar point about the understanding of racial differences and the acquisition of positive and negative feelings about racial groups. Babette Brown (2001) describes how the use of Persona Dolls with children of this age can support all the children in understanding the effects of prejudice and discrimination. This is important because racism inflicts damage on all children, whatever their racial or cultural background. For white children it affects their ability to reason, distorts judgements and perceptions of reality, and gives them a false sense of self. For children from minority ethnic backgrounds it may undermine children's self-esteem and self-confidence. There is known to be a correlation between high self-esteem and high academic performance (Purkey 1970).

To give all children a message of acceptance means valuing the experience each of them brings to a setting. This includes experiences that are often not highly valued in society in general such as being poor, being a refugee, being working class or from a single parent or lesbian or gay family – experiences that are often invisible in children's books, songs and play environments. If, as we have noted, babies and young children have experience of a social world that is much wider than has previously been acknowledged and that they absorb at an early age the culture and beliefs of the society in which they live, the implications for those working and living with children from birth to three are huge. Thinking about how practitioners can offer continuity of experience to the baby or young child, whose culture and home values may be different from those practitioners are familiar with, takes on more importance. Practitioners must, therefore, constantly reflect on their practice and the assumptions they make that underpin it.

Understanding others

The perceptual abilities that babies are born with, and rapidly develop after birth, seem to predispose them to be a part of the social world into which they are born. Babies' hearing is well developed and they are tuned into voices, particularly their mothers, which they have been listening to while still in the womb. Babies' tracking reflex allows them to follow movement and they are particularly interested in human movement. Although the least well developed of all the senses, a small baby's vision is able to focus on the adult's face when held in the crook of the arm or fed at the breast and again they are particularly tuned in to the shape and contours of the human face (Gopnik *et al.* 1999).

These abilities form the basis upon which the young child builds their growing understanding of other people's different thoughts and feelings as they play together. This is an understanding that is unique to humans, often referred to as having theory of mind. This knowledge underpins all our relationships (Gopnik *et al.* 1999; Bee 2000). As adults we draw on a lifetime's experience of feelings and other people's responses to gauge someone's likely response in varying situations and even then can get it wrong. Children up to 3 are at the very beginning of life-long learning in the school of social relationships and are finding out about others in their play.

Very young babies can interpret adults' emotional expressions. If they meet with a blank or depressed expression they become upset and try to disengage from the interaction by averting their gaze (Trevarthan 1993). Babies are interested in each other from an early age; they watch each other at play, gazing at others' faces, moving their mouths and making arm and leg movements in response to each other. They also respond to other babies' cries and become upset themselves; this is a familiar situation to practitioners working with babies in groups, where one baby after another begins to cry.

Babies show an increasing understanding of appropriate expressions and contexts as they refer back to their parent or key person, checking the adult's expression to see if a play situation is okay or whether what they are about to do is permissible. Young toddlers watch another's tears with fascination, apparently veering between scientific study and crying themselves. However as their own sense of self is more firmly established, as reflected in their mirror play, toddlers show empathic understanding of other's feelings. They may offer a tissue to an upset friend or comment on another's feelings. Judy Dunn shows how remarkably adept at perceiving, predicting and responding to the feelings of baby siblings children up to 3 years are even though their language skills are limited (1988).

> In the baby room 4-month-old Asha is fretful. Billie (16 months) rocks her in her lie-back chair until she settles.

Young children's ability to empathize seems to be also linked to their own sense of security. Those who are securely attached to a significant other are more likely to be able to share other people's feelings (Talay-Ongen 1998).

On the fluctuating seesaw of a toddler's social and emotional life, however, showing empathy is frequently out-balanced by the toddler's own overriding needs. Toddlers are still learning what it means to be 'me' and therefore they are not able to consistently consider or understand others' needs. This means they are not able to fully grasp social concepts such as sharing, although they are good at distributing and collecting. For example:

> Matilda (2 years) has a bag of Duplo bricks, which she distributes to each of the children in the home corner. Most of the other children are not particularly interested when she collects them all back again but Rosie protests. The practitioner reaches across to the Duplo on the rug and offers both of them an extra brick.

Toddlers often enjoy the company of other children and they follow each other and imitate each other's play, laughing together when their goals coincide. However, their still limited social skills mean that they will tussle over the space or a particular toy as soon as their needs conflict. Toddlers who are trying to communicate their needs and emotions with a limited vocabulary can feel very frustrated, especially if frequently misunderstood or misinterpreted. They already have strong emotions and if they are unable to express themselves verbally then physical means are a logical way for 18-month-olds to get what they want. Sometimes they appear callous as they look at the crying child they have just pushed over, but toddlers are fascinated by the results of their actions, including their social relationships.

Toddlers may feign crying in such a situation, apparently to avoid censure. In other situations they may use a range of put-on emotions to try to persuade the adult to take them to the park or let them have a biscuit. Parents and practitioners sometimes see this behaviour as deception or manipulation, which to a degree it is but the intent is not malevolent. Practising these behaviours in their play helps toddlers to learn how to influence people, a skill needed throughout our lives.

Whatever the ups and downs, toddlers often make good friends with whom they play for long periods, especially when they have similar interests, and these friendships can last a long time. Where toddlers have long-term relationships with the same group of peers they tend to be more popular and more socially interactive in the childcare setting (Lieberman 1993). These observations of young children should make us think carefully about how practitioners organize groupings of children in nursery settings.

Developing a sense of autonomy

In early toddlerhood three aspects of development combine to bring about a revolution in the toddler's self-concept. Independent movement means the toddler can determine when and where to go. A consolidated understanding of object and person permanence gives greater confidence in playing away from the adult and a clearer idea of self means that they start to make choices and decisions. These changes impact significantly on the way toddlers like to play.

In contrast to dependent, compliant babies, mobile toddlers have their own agenda of what they want (and do not want) to play with and where they want to go and when. When these desires coincide with those of the parent or key person, there is harmony. When they do not, there is potential conflict. In the second year of life, only about 50 per cent of parental requests are initially complied with by toddlers (Lieberman 1993).

When the differing goals of child and adult can be reconciled through negotiation, the relationship becomes a partnership where there is enough flexibility to reach a compromise. Toddlers' new found social abilities are as yet unrefined, however, often resulting in opposition, negativism and temper tantrums as toddlers quite naturally want to put their needs first (Lieberman 1993). These new skills require practice in different play situations, repetition to refine them and support and guidance from more experienced others to develop them appropriately. The practitioner's task is to find a way of moving away from confrontation and a battle of wills to negotiation.

A common area of possible conflict between adults and young children arises from their different understanding of time and end goals. For example:

> Miranda's goal might be reaching the post office before it closes but this is irrelevant to Nathan who operates in the here and now, not the future. Like all toddlers he is fascinated with process and detail, therefore he is more interested in walking on the wall and watching the trail of ants on the pavement. When Miranda tries to hurry him along he pulls away from her hand and sits down on the pavement, refusing to move.

Toddlers are so keen to practise their ability to make choices and decisions that they may say no to something that they want or refuse help with something they clearly cannot yet do. They also frequently change their minds. Practitioners will be familiar with the child who touches every piece of fruit on the offered plate before choosing and even then change their mind. It takes time to learn to cope with having choices. The more practice toddlers get at choosing, for example from a range of accessible play materials, the more able they become.

In the process of exploring their autonomy and independence, toddlers encounter a social world that can be very confusing. Children make tremendous gains in understanding in their first three years. However their understanding in relation to social rules is only at the beginning:

> When Rhys plays pouring and filling with pots in the water tray he receives much adult approval. Later on, in the bathroom he continues this action with a feeder cup in the toilet and looks bewildered by the adult's horrified response.

Sometimes in these situations toddlers appear to understand what is unacceptable behaviour and resist temptation but other times they seem to completely forget. This is not surprising when we consider how much they are learning at this time.

Toddlers' ability to regulate their feelings is slowly developing. The process of myelination, that strengthens the connections in the brain, is coating the neurons responsible for affective regulation at this time, a process that is not fully completed until early adulthood (Eliot 1999). They often show remarkable self-control but also sometimes lose control of themselves in an emotional collapse, either through being overwhelmed or frustrated.

Some tantrums are a learnt means to get attention or something the toddler wants that may have proved to be very effective. An adult may be tempted to be very critical of the toddler for this. A more positive approach to this is to help the child realize that it is not effective in this group and to show her/him what is effective. For example:

Amin (2) wanted to go on the trip to the library barefoot and was on the floor crying.

Adam: I know you like being barefoot, but the stones outside will hurt your feet. You can stay here and play with your shoes off or put them on and come with us. Which do you want to do?
Amin: Go with no shoes.
Adam: Sorry that's not a choice. I tell you what. You can wear your own nice trainers or you can wear these nice red nursery wellies. You choose and put them on while we go and put our names in the outing book, but we can only wait five minutes for you.

Amin put on the wellington boots and joined the group.

As Mckay acknowledges it takes careful discernment to know whether a tantrum is an emotional collapse due to cumulative frustrations or a ploy for getting the toddler's wants supplied. She goes on to say: 'Caregivers tend to overuse the excuse that a tantrum is a bid for attention . . . Most young children are frightened when their emotions get out of hand and usually need comfort and reassurance' (Mckay in Stonehouse 1988: 72).

Anne Stonehouse (1988) describes toddlers as 'person creating' and that this involves the following:

- finding out that they are a separate person;
- becoming more self-sufficient;
- coping with freedom and choices;
- learning that actions have consequences;
- learning how to influence and to persuade people;
- resisting coercion from authority.

We continue to use and relearn these lessons at times of change and transition throughout our lives. If a child has sensitive adult support in understanding these social tasks in the first three years they will be better equipped to manage difficult times in later life (Manning-Morton and Thorp 2000).

Playing with others

Perspectives on social play

Mildred Parten's (1932) description of the development of peer play is, like Piaget's, set out in stages. The first step she defined as solitary play. Babies engage in solitary play exploring their environment on their own. They may come into contact with other children but more as objects to explore rather than interact with. This develops into parallel play. Children engaged in parallel play, play alongside each other; they may watch each other closely, and imitate each other too but that is the extent of their interaction. By the end of the third year, Parten described children as engaging in associative play. They may play together but each has their own agenda. All is well until they both want to use the same piece of equipment. Others can join their play as long as it is on their terms. Finally cooperative play emerges. Children engaged in cooperative play work together on shared projects and imaginative games. They listen to each other's ideas and negotiate what roles each will play.

Play with others is primary.

Tina Bruce questions this concept of the development of peer play being a 'simple to complex ladder of hierarchy' (Bruce and Meggitt 1996: 207). She describes a gradually spreading web as a better analogy. Bruce gives the examples of early associative and cooperative play between babies such as peek-a-boo games and of solitary and parallel play between older children.

Catherine Garvey says that play with others is primary and that solitary play is derived from this (Garvey 1990). A baby's first social play is with their primary caregiver, a large part of which consists of creating humorous situations in which the baby will smile and laugh. Much of what we find humorous as adults is incongruity, that is, something that is unexpected, and very young babies already share this kind of humour. As long as they are in a non-threatening context, they will laugh at things that are distorted or exaggerated, such as the adult pulling a funny face or pretending to drop the banana. Babies actively participate in and sustain these games and as they mature they actively produce behaviours that generate amusement. Familiarity of surroundings is crucial to this response; babies do not smile in a strange situation or with an unfamiliar adult, although they may smile at an unknown child.

Making contact with others in play

Babies' play with familiar adults is regulated by the attunement of the adult and their play with objects is controlled by their own actions. Their play with other children, however, is less controllable and predictable. Their success depends on the growing social skill of understanding others and balancing their own and others' desires and also on sensitive adult support. Children from birth to three are more confident in their approaches to other children when a familiar adult is present.

The play of babies and toddlers is also often described as moving in stages from play with objects to play with other children, implying that there is little interest in other children before this. The work of Goldschmied and Selleck (1996) shows how very young babies respond to each other with movements and vocalizations. They also show how objects are not only explored by the individual child but are used in games of give and take with adults and other children as a form of communication where a child has yet few words. Young children can develop friendships and express kindness and concern through offering objects and in imitating each others' use of a similar object, develop a shared, exclusive ritual in their play (Goldschmied and Selleck 1996).

As adults we find out about each other through talking (although we also play squash or do patchwork together); for young children play is their talk. In play a toddler's actions do not carry the same consequences as usual; young children can make mistakes and take risks in their interactions as play partners are usually more tolerant. Therefore learning about others and self in a play situation is safer. So as well as exploring and testing the physical world, young children are learning how to convey their thoughts and intentions and to understand the communications of others in their play.

Social pretend play

Generally children's ability to play socially with other children is seen to emerge at about 3 years old when they engage in cooperative pretend play. For Vygotsky (1966) the ability to separate meaning from object, such as by using a block to stand for a hairbrush, and create imaginary situations is the criterion for play. This, he says is impossible for children from birth to three as their actions are dictated by the properties of the object. This contrasts starkly with Winnicott's (1971) description of young children's creation of transitional objects. Göncü (1993) challenges Vygotsky's view, describing the gradually developing ability of toddlers to cooperate in pretend play.

The earliest forms of social pretend play are based on the child sharing experiences with peers that are emotionally significant; these are often centred around a theme such as caring for babies and so are frequently shared experiences in which both children find meaning. The limited language of toddlers means these intentions are often communicated through exaggerated movements, gestures and facial expressions. At first 15- to 20-month-olds will mirror each other's pretend actions, then these actions become more sequenced as they interact. Then, through the third year children begin to engage in the same play theme and adopt complementary roles. Judy Dunn (1988) also describes the participation of children from 18 months of age in pretend play with their siblings. She notes that children who play with older siblings in an affectionate relationship tend to be more cooperative at 3 years old. From these observations it seems that engaging in social pretend play coincides with the child's ability to use symbolic representations, which Piaget described as emerging towards the end of the sensory-motor stage of development (1962).

In a Piagetian framework of play, the symbolic play stage is followed by games with rules. Rather than being a later stage of play, however, it has been pointed out that games with rules also exist in children's play from the beginning. Peek-a-boo is not only a universal game in which babies interact with others, explore concepts on an emotional and cognitive level such as object and person permanence, make-believe and real, but a game in which babies also quickly learn the 'rules' of the game and its sequence (Bruner and Sherwood 1975).

Implications for practice

The type of peer play children engage in is influenced not just by the ages of the children. There are many other factors, for example:

- their experience of being with peers;
- the amount of language a child has;
- how well children know each other;
- the size of the group;
- how the child is feeling, physically or emotionally;
- the support of the adults.

In fact these are just the same factors that influence adults' ability to function in groups. The role of the practitioner is to be sensitive to the children as individuals, and to try to understand what factors are influencing each child's play. As Bruce and Meggitt (1996) point out, forcing children to share equipment when the ideas that are driving their play are separate does not make sense. They give an example of two children playing together in the home corner. One has the idea of laying the table, the other of mixing pancakes. A cook's work surface and a laid table cannot be one and the same thing! So the adult's role should be to ensure another table or an alternative work surface is found, to enable children to enjoy their peer play more.

Smolucha's (1991) research indicated that their mothers' modelling this type of play influence the age at which children start using objects to represent other things. Furthermore Slade (1987) found that the length of episodes of symbolic/pretend play, and the complexity of this play, is greater when mothers are available to play with their 12- to 24-month-old children. These findings suggest a toddler's ability to engage in pretend play is expanded by the involvement and support of those caring for them.

In terms of supporting children's self-concept, practitioners may see children's play as preparation for their future roles in life rather than as helping them to make meaning of and integrate their experiences (Bruce 1991). This may lead adults to restrict certain kinds of play or react adversely according to their own beliefs of what are desirable roles, particularly in relation to gender, for example disapproving of boys dressing up or of girls running and shouting. The complexity of pretend or symbolic play that a child is able to engage in has a direct correlation with their ability to think. Therefore we need to consider carefully the role of practitioner as play partner and the messages practitioners give children about valuing or devaluing their chosen theme of play.

The adult's role in supporting the social play of children from birth to three ∎

Knowledge and understanding about young children's personal and social development and behaviour allows those working with children from birth to three to be more able:

- to plan appropriate play experiences;
- to empathize and negotiate with children in play scenarios;
- to support diversity and challenge bias in play provision;
- to be more likely to experience job satisfaction.

Being a role model

Toddlers are constantly looking to those who care for them for how to react to new situations. They are already picking up clues of how to respond to others with different languages, skin tones, abilities and gender. They are watching how their key workers relate to other children, parents/carers and colleagues and learning how they should relate to these people from what they see. They learn not only from the adult's conscious overt comments and behaviours but also from adults' silences, averted gazes and avoided subjects.

In relation to diversity, everyone has areas they feel less or more comfortable about but it is the practitioner's responsibility, whatever their own cultural or religious background, to educate themselves about different lifestyles and to impart a message of interest and ease about difference to the children. Where practitioners observe children having having difficulties, story sessions using Persona Dolls (Brown 2001) can help children to understand each other's feelings and perspectives.

Developing a shared approach though play

Sharing information with parents about the children's languages and cultures allows the practitioner to weave them into children's play in a meaningful context. If a key person is able to use important words in each child's home language and is knowledgeable about significant events in the child's cultural and religious life, the child's sense of continuity between home and setting will be enhanced.

Practitioners need to feel confident to talk openly with children about the similarities and differences of ethnicity, gender, ability and family amongst the children in the group and in the wider community. It is also important to agree with parents the use of proper words for genital body parts and bodily products. Not only will this support the children's self-knowledge but will also contribute to the setting's child protection practice. To do these things practitioners need time to explore their personal and professional values and opportunities for training and discussion about valuing diversity and anti-bias practice.

Supporting friendships through play

Practitioners who support young children's social skills effectively focus on enabling the children to enjoy each other's company in play as an important aspect of their role. They value children's play together by placing and holding babies in ways that will support the interactions between them and by being involved in the children's play, offering suggestions and useful language to help children express their wants, needs and ideas to each other. It is important that practitioners know about their key children's friendships and plan play experiences and routine times to support these. Toddlers often approach babies and each other clumsily, but will learn appropriate methods if practitioners model the behaviours they expect of the children when playing together, such as negotiating, respect for and gentle handling of others.

Appreciating positive behaviour

By knowing the children's relationships with one another and being close at hand a practitioner can anticipate possible conflict in play and draw children's attention to what they can do, not just what they cannot do. This helps to avoid overuse of the word 'no'. If practitioners want children to develop their positive behaviours they need to let them know what they are. Effective practice in this respect means showing children appreciation of their efforts at pro-social behaviour, specifically identifying the behaviour and its

By being close at hand and involved in play, practitioners can anticipate conflict and model pro-social behaviour.

positive consequences. Noticing and making positive comments on children's acts of kindness and care towards others and the environment when they are playing helps them to understand their behaviours and its effects more precisely.

Partnership

A key characteristic of practitioners working with babies and toddlers is that they are interested in working in partnership with toddlers, not having power over them. Having a partnership approach to children's social play means that practitioners are more able to cope light-heartedly with a toddler's unpredictability and are less likely to get into battle of wills situations. They empathize when toddlers' early attempts at assertion and negotiation go wrong, acknowledging and verbalizing the children's good and bad feelings. By knowing their key children well practitioners are able to tell when conflict in play arises from tiredness or misunderstanding, so are able to show fairness and apply rules flexibly and reasonably, giving children an alternative wherever possible. They are consistent so as to provide clear boundaries yet do not adhere to the kind of consistency where an adult will not back down from a decision, even though it was mistaken or unnecessary. They show willingness to change their minds in the face of other evidence, as this teaches children about the value of engaging in dialogue and negotiation and about differing points of view (Lieberman 1993). The empathy and fairness of the adult's response can help children to find acceptable ways to assert themselves. They will learn alternatives to using physical means, or to just giving in.

In a partnership approach, a practitioner is also prepared to reflect on their own part in the overall level of difficult behaviour amongst a group of children. If babies and toddlers are frequently 'falling apart' in a group then the practitioner will first re-evaluate the routines of the day, the physical environment and the play experiences available to check whether they are supporting the children or not. They will also monitor whether the children have their key person consistently available, providing them with a secure base.

Supporting the development of self-discipline

Discipline, guiding children's behaviour, or setting limits are all concerned with helping children learn how to take care of themselves, other people and the world around them.

(Greenman and Stonehouse 1996: 138)

By implementing the practices outlined above, practitioners will be operating along the whole continuum of practice that guides the behaviour of children from birth to three. By playing in partnership or remaining available to support babies' and toddlers' social play, practitioners can provide the guidance that helps children to develop inner control. In *Key Times* (Manning-Morton and Thorp 2001) the authors outline many ways in which practitioners can do this. Fundamental to developing an agreed approach to guiding children's behaviour is the practitioners' understanding of the degree to which their own childhood experiences influence their approach. Adults are annoyed, disgusted or frustrated by different behaviours and will have been allowed to do, and punished for, different things in different ways in their early years. The more a practitioner can identify why particular behaviours bother them and the benefits or problems associated with the way they were disciplined, the more measured they can be in their responses to children. This must include reflection on their responses to particular behaviours as shown by different children; are they consistent between boys and girls, between children from all racial and ethnic backgrounds between able and disabled children? Are they more flexible with some and more negative with others?

> When we did the exercise about children's behaviour, I realised that although things like biting and hitting upset me, the thing that really irritates me is when children are just passive and don't stand up for themselves. I have had to do a lot of thinking about why this pushes my buttons so much and realised that because I was bullied when I was young I don't want these children to remind me of how that felt. Now I know that, I can temper the way I react in those situations.
> (Manning-Morton and Thorp 2001: sect. 5, p. 8)

In fraught situations practitioners also need to contain and reduce their own feelings of stress. If, however, they are struggling with a situation or are losing control, leaving the situation and seeking help is the wise thing to do. Some practitioners may feel that not being able to manage in every difficult situation is a failure on their part and consequently persist in dealing with a child when it is not in their own or the child's best interests. Therefore it is necessary to develop an organizational culture in which practitioners can see that recognizing one's own limitations and vulnerabilities is a strength and where they can discuss difficulties with a supportive manager. This may help to avoid potentially dangerous situations for children and to reduce staff burnout.

Positive experiences of companionable play ■

Finding out about each other in play

The video *Communication between Babies in Their First Year* (Gold-schmied and Selleck 1996) shows the intense interest very young babies have in watching and touching each other. Placing non-mobile babies so they can see and touch each other facilitates this interest. They will also be interested in looking at themselves if laid beside a low-level mirror. This video also shows how babies and toddlers enjoy rolling over and climbing on each other in a way that is reminiscent of puppies. This rough and tumble play helps young children to explore their physical strength and learn about variations in acceptability of physical interaction with different people. Practitioners observing babies playing in this way should resist the urge to rescue a baby being climbed on unless there are signals of distress. Attentive practitioners will be able to facilitate both fun and gentleness as babies and toddlers tumble together.

Outdoor play

Outdoor play provides great opportunities for practising and refining physical skills providing the outdoor play space is appropriately equipped. However, a wider significance of outdoor play was observed and documented by the staff of one birth to threes unit (Rowlett 2000). It was noted that the trikes, trucks and wheeled toys in general were very popular. Close observation over a period of time showed that the toddlers passed through three distinct stages. The first was indeed to master the physical skills needed for controlling a trike, push-along truck or pram. The second was to imitate other slightly more proficient wheeled-toy users. Practitioners observed several toddlers following each other on a specific route round the garden. The third stage was to be the leader and to incorporate pretend play. One child was seen to be dictating when and where the convoy should go (as in the observation of Raj in Chapter 3). Leaders were seen to stop and declare a picnic or that they were at a station. This gave practitioners an insight into the value of wheeled toys and the need for there to be plenty of them. Prior to this they had undervalued bike play.

Children's experience of social roles such as being a leader or follower will also be influenced by other aspects. For example:

Sam (just 3 years old) has not had use of his left arm since birth. When playing outside with his friends he was unable to experience being in a leader role as controlling a trike with one hand meant he was not as fast at racing up and down as the others. This was a source of sadness and frustration for him. His mum then found a specially adapted scooter that could be controlled with one hand. Now not only could Sam go as fast as his friends, he found that he was the object of their envy and admiration as they all wanted a turn on his scooter but found that they were not as adept as controlling it as Sam was. Sam was now in a position to sometimes take on a leader role in this particular game.

Visits, outings and projects

Adults go to classes, go on organized trips and do voluntary work knowing that doing interesting things with others builds friendships and provides a wealth of material for later recall and enjoyment. There will be funny, unexpected happenings, new discoveries and scary moments to recount. Babies and toddlers can also enjoy these benefits by participating in outings, having visitors come to their group or going off to do a 'job' together. The success of these activities will depend on how finely tuned they are to the age of children participating. Babies and toddlers will gain a lot more from them if the group is small. For example:

> Four children and two adults went on a bus ride to a local pet shop. They took a camera, some water and bought some bananas from the greengrocer's stall near the pet shop. This trip was full of memorable happenings. The little photograph album of the trip was often looked at and the children loved to recall how the parrot could talk but even more interestingly that Andy (the student) had a nose bleed!

The larger the number participating and the more complex the journey, the more stressful it becomes for adults as well as children and the more conversation there will be about control and safety rather than discussion of what children are seeing and doing.

Opportunities for babies and toddlers to find out about others can be created by visitors bringing their pet to the nursery, fire-fighters coming with their engines, a musician playing their instrument or a parent bathing a new baby in the group room. However, contingency plans need to be in place, for there is always the possibility that at least one baby or toddler will be fearful of this new experience or person; also children's interest will only be sustained if there is an active part for them to play.

Role re-plays

Older toddlers and 2-year-olds will enjoy pretend play that is about people or events they know well or have recently experienced. Multi-purpose resources like cut down net curtains, plastic flowers, bow ties, shoes and waistcoats can help children to recreate family celebrations, like bar mitzvahs and weddings. Some discussion with parents will provide enough detail to make it realistic. Hard hats and lengths of hose can enable children to recall and play at being fire-fighters. Blocks set out in a square with water wings will encourage a re-play of going swimming. When based on recent events, these play experiences are meaningful and relevant to the children in the group and provide opportunities to include different family events, cultures and religious practices.

Toddlers enjoy pretend play that is about people or events they know well.

Play in small groups

As adults, we do not like to be constantly one of a crowd of 12 or more people; we also need cosier times with two or three close friends. Yet this is the size of many groups of children from birth to three, who also need to have times with few people, especially as the size of the group affects the quality of their play.

If practitioners ensure children spend some time playing in small groups each day with their key worker, the children will be able to experience an environment with less bustle. These may be lively times with action songs and games or quiet, chatty, intimate times like sharing a book or photo album together. They can be times special treasures are explored as in Goldschmied and Jackson's 'islands of intimacy' (1994: 41, 135).

Duplicates

Duplicate materials provide babies and toddlers with opportunities to imitate and learn from each other without conflict. This includes having two or three types of popular resource sets with many components rather than a lot of different sets but with only a small number of items in each. This concept of duplicates extends to the book corner. We have discussed adults and children sharing stories; having duplicates of popular books enable the children to share stories together too.

The play resources mentioned throughout this book are largely those that are collections of everyday things, for example bags, containers, boxes, corks and pieces of material. These are well suited to foster good social experiences for young children as well as promoting physical and creative skills. They are open ended to allow children to play with them differently according to whether they wish to be alone, play alongside others or play collaboratively with a friend. Just as adults need time to be alone and work or play uninterrupted, babies' and toddlers' attempts to play undisturbed should be respected too, and not be mistaken as a children 'not sharing'.

5

CHILDREN FROM BIRTH TO THREE COMMUNICATING AND PLAYING

Playing and communicating in meaningful contexts

Lydia (23 months) has found a box of laminated characters that Ruth (her childminder) uses for storytelling. She takes them out one by one, and hands them to Ruth, and putting her face right in front of Ruth's says a great deal of completely incomprehensible sounds that sound very much like adult conversation. She waits expectantly.

Ruth: Yes this is Peter. Do you remember, Peter went in a boat?
Lydia: Mummy sick.
Ruth: Poor Mummy was seasick when you went to France on holiday.
Lydia: All better now.
Ruth: Yes, Mummy's not sick any more.

Lydia crosses the room and holds Peter behind the radiator. Looking at Ruth, she lets go.

Ruth: Oh dear where's Peter? He's gone behind the radiator. Bye bye Peter, going down.

This game is repeated many times. Soon Lydia is saying the refrain and naming each character. Then one of the characters goes behind the loose wallpaper at the back of the radiator and so does not fall to the carpet as Lydia is expecting it to.

Lydia: Zaccus gone. Ruth do it!
Ruth: Do you want me to try and get Zacchaeus out?

Lydia pats the air palms down, the sign accompanying a song about Zacchaeus. Ruth sings the song, joining in the actions.

Lydia: Ruth do it. (She takes Ruth's hand and brings her to the radiator.)
Ruth: I can't see where he is. Let's get the torch.

Lydia knows about the torch, this isn't the first time she has used it. She runs into the kitchen and points to the shelf in the cupboard. But then Lydia hears a lawnmower start up in a nearby garden; she looks worried.

Lydia: Wadawada on! (Wadawada is her name for anything that goes round and round and has a motor. Lydia is both fascinated by and wary of wadawadas.)
Ruth: Can you hear the lawnmower? Its OK, it's outside in the garden.
Lydia: In the garden, wadawada! (She points at the window and looks at Ruth.)
Ruth: Do you want to see the lawnmower? (Ruth goes to the back door. Lydia stands frowning.)
Lydia: Wadawada up! (She points at the window.)
Ruth: Oh you want to look at the lawnmower through the window. It is very noisy isn't it? But it won't hurt you. It just cuts the grass.

She lifts Lydia up to the window and they watch their neighbour mowing for a while, chatting about how the birds and cats have all gone because they don't like the noise. Lydia looks down at the radiator her feet are resting on; she struggles to get down.

Lydia: Torch, down.

They get the torch and the search for the trapped Zacchaeus recommences.

Vygotsky argued that a mastery of language is synonymous with an effectual capacity to think. His dialectical theory is that discussion and dialogue bring about new ways of thinking (Vygotsky 1986). Halliday (1975) described talk as a means to satisfy our needs and desires, to control or be controlled and to establish and maintain contact; it facilitates our expression of ideas and thoughts, helps us to find things out, to create worlds and to represent. This is apparent in the observation above of Lydia. Therefore any help we give babies and young children to become competent, confident talkers through their play has a positive impact on all other areas of development.

Communicating and playing from birth

Babies are communicators from birth. They are able to recognize human voices they have heard in the womb and after birth they pay more attention to human voices than other auditory stimuli (Karmiloff-Smith 1995). Manning-Morton and Thorp (2001) itemize the many and varied ways even very young babies are able to express their needs and feelings. By crying they communicate their fear, pain, hunger, boredom or loneliness. They gaze, smile, reach, laugh and point to communicate interest and amusement. Babies stare, break eye-contact, grimace and arch their bodies to express their displeasure and warn strangers not to come closer.

Bruner (1977) observed the pre-linguistic behaviour of babies when interacting and playing with their carers. He saw that:

• babies soon recognize adult intentions;
• they engage in turn-taking behaviour;
• they develop an awareness of rituals around actions and language;
• they learn to make links between objects and language.

From his observations Bruner believed the basic schemas for developing language begin very early in life. He suggests that early social games and interactions help babies grasp the turn-taking form of conversation, and how this is a rich means of giving and receiving information. He believed a lot of learning took place around familiar routines (Bruner 1977). Consequently it is important for those caring for very young children to be tuned in to their gestures and vocalizations. This responsiveness and attentiveness needs to be both physical and verbal because of the significant learning that is taking place during nappy changing, sleep and mealtime routines. Walking up and down with a baby on the shoulder, rocking, or gently massaging a baby, are all ways of communicating that underpin early language development.

Different traditions support language development in diverse ways, through responsive vocal interactions or through more direct modelling and instruction for example. Therefore it is important for

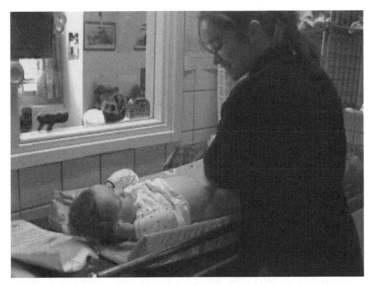

*Routine care times are prime times for communicating one
to one.*

practitioners to be aware of the substantial differences in approaches
to fostering linguistic skills in different homes. They need to be clear
that there is a stark difference between the children of attentive
parents/carers who are tuned in to their children and play with them,
yet have different cultural approaches to language development,
and children who have been in isolation, in sole contact with very
depressed caregivers or those experiencing neglect or abuse.

Learning to talk, learning to play

By approximately 6 months old babies may have begun to babble;
these are early vowel sounds interspersed by consonants. By the end
of the first year intonation, imitative of adult talk, can be detected
and this begins to convey meaning. Increased lip and tongue
coordination enables more complex sounds to be produced, and
children with different mother tongues sound different now. Bates
describes this as 'learning the tune before the words' (Bates *et al.* 1987,
cited in Bee 2000: 230). However, long before this difference in babies'
vocalization is detectable, babies show that they hear the difference
between their home language and any other. This has been detected
in babies at 4 days old (Karmiloff-Smith 1994). Parents/carers often
respond enthusiastically to their babies' 'talk', attributing meaning to

these sounds. This language play encourages babies to repeat the sounds they hear, link sound to meaning and provides language models.

In the baby's second year individual words are formed, but simplified to enable pronunciation. Consonants are sounded just at the beginning of words at first, then middle, and gradually end consonants are sounded. Consonant clusters are simplified, unstressed syllables are left out and syllables are duplicated. At this time pretend play emerges. Receptive language development, that is, making sense of language is also progressing. Toddlers hearing a string of sounds, try to segment them into identifiable chunks; in doing so they tend to overextend word meanings. They also overgeneralize their use of words and they echo the last word/s of what adults say to them, as we saw from the observation of Lydia and the wadawada. By this age toddlers also understand and use a wealth of facial expressions and gestures as they play.

Once walking the toddler's world really opens up and single words to describe objects and actions are used often with accompanying gestures. In addition to the 20 or so words the toddler may be able to say, their understanding may be of 40–100 words. The toddlers' words may not be well pronounced but, as they converse and play, they may use a variety of 'protolanguage' sounds that vary in pitch, volume, and intonation (Trevarthan 1979).

> Lydia's parents describe her use of protolanguage as: 'long "conversations" with us that are completely incomprehensible yet sound exactly like adult talk. She also puts her face close to ours and looks intently at the person she is talking to.'

By approximately 2 to 3 years old children begin to form sentences and use telegraphic speech, with sentences that contain just the key words. An example of this is Lydia's 'Ruth do it'. Language development is often rapid now; there is an explosion of new vocabulary; plurals, pronouns and adjectives all emerge and grammar errors show the child's growing understanding of grammatical rules. However, thinking and strength of feeling can go faster than the child's ability to say things. This can result in stuttering or physical expressions of frustration. Elinor Goldschmied gives practitioners the following advice.

> When feelings and ideas come faster than words, a child will often stutter in eagerness. It helps if the worker gently holds the child's hand, and if others are clamouring for attention, asks for

a bit of quiet, showing her genuine consideration for what the child is struggling to say.

(Goldschmied and Jackson 1994: 135–6)

In the third year, 'private speech' (Vygotsky 1986) or what Piaget described as 'egocentric' speech (1926) also emerges. Children may seem to be talking to themselves as they play. For example Callum was heard to say to no one in particular when playing in the garden, 'Ball gone in the bushes, Callum get stick.' These single or collective monologues, that are not attempts to converse with others, were regarded by Piaget as a sign of the pre-operational child's immaturity. Vygotsky saw 'private speech' as a child's way of planning and directing their actions, of problem solving, the sort of thinking out loud adults are known to do on occasions. Private speech gradually becomes inaudible and Vygotsky viewed it as a precursor to the ability for internal thought (1986).

Although our focus is birth to 3-year-olds it is important to know what to expect next in terms of development, as children vary greatly. By approximately 3 to 4 years old the child will be frequently asking 'why' questions. They will be able to talk about the past, and speculate about the future more easily and specifically.

Playing, communicating and talking

Communicating, talking and playing with peers

Babies and toddlers are able to communicate and initiate play with each other by gesture, imitation and by playing with the same materials long before language is acquired. Recent research has identified that babies, still too physically immature to speak, can learn to use gesture and sign to communicate their needs. Babies who learnt to sign were found to engage in more complex play, had increased cognitive development, and at 2 years had more language than non-signing peers (Acredolo and Goodwyn 2000). Some practitioners are wary of signing unless a child is identified as having particular special needs, thinking that this will delay the onset of language. Yet Acredolo and Goodwyn (2000) point out that a young child's readiness and enthusiasm for signing is obvious from their participation in action songs long before they can sing the words. Pointing, waving goodbye, nodding and shaking their heads are just some of the very early signs they saw that almost all babies use.

In Acredolo and Goodwyn's research (1985), parents/carers who sign with their 1 to 2-year-olds reported many benefits. Their toddlers experienced less frustration as signing enabled them to communicate, thereby enhancing the relationships between parents/carers and their children and between peers. An example given is one toddler witnessing the distress of a toddler friend on separating from her mother at nursery. She used her sign for fish to her sobbing friend. The practitioner noticing this realized she was encouraging the child to go and feed the fish, an activity often used to console upset children (Acredolo and Goodwyn 2000).

Communicating and playing with close adults

We have identified how, in the first three years, children's language usually develops rapidly. This is influenced by the quality of the relationship between the baby and close adults. Karmiloff-Smith (1994) says that the sensitivity of the parents/carers to their baby in the first few months of life has a direct correlation to the linguistic ability of the baby at 12 months. An example of this is the parent/carer or practitioner who rewards a baby's vocal play with their attention and willingness to enter into the game.

Trevarthan describes babies as young as 2 months being interested in engaging in these protoconversations or communication games by

Babies and carers co-ordinate their gestures and expressions in communication games.

responding with gestures and expressions that are coordinated with the carer's contributions (Trevarthan 1979). The rhythm of conversation can be detected even with very young babies who suck vigorously when feeding, then pause, gazing at the carer. The carer can be observed to chat in the pauses and gently jiggle the baby who recommences sucking. Trevarthan argues that babies' linguistic development and therefore cognitive development is clearly shaped by the quality of the protoconversations between themselves and their close carers; moreover he emphasizes the central role that emotions and their communication have in cognitive growth (1995). He believes that babies' protoconversations with their close carers in the first 3 months can provide the essential motivation that enables children to enter nursery with a huge fund of cultural knowledge and wide vocabulary (Trevarthan 1979, 1993, 1995). The imitative play described in Chapter 2 fosters this motivation.

Trevarthan observed that at 3 months babies show great interest in toys their carers show them, and are fascinated by the 'vocal gloss' of the carer's voice even though they are as yet unable to intentionally grasp the object or understand the words accompanying this play (1995, in Woodhead *et al.* 1998: 91). They communicate this interest with grunts, sighs and squeals.

Many parents/carers (who have not had any schooling in language acquisition) automatically engage in verbal play with their babies. They develop their own special way of conversing with their babies, which is much richer and more meaningful than words alone. They use facial expressions, tone, pitch and gesture as they play and 'chat'. Research into what has come to be called 'Motherese' or 'Child Directed Speech' has been found to be very sensitive to the child's communicative abilities and stays one step ahead of the child's current capabilities (Bohannon and Warren-Leubecker 1988). This speech has shorter sentences, and has a restricted vocabulary. It uses exaggerated intonation, attention-getting prompts and is of a higher pitch (Fernald *et al.* 1989). It occurs in almost all cultures and language communities, including among deaf parents/carers who sign to their children (Bee 2000). Words mean far less if their meaning is not also communicated by facial expression, tone, pitch and gesture.

Playing with words and sounds

Just as babies and young children play with other newly acquired skills and knowledge, so they play with their new resources of vocalizations and language (Garvey 1990). At the babbling stage, babies will repeat different combinations of sounds at varying pitch levels. For example:

> Billie's favourite combinations were a mixture of aba abu da da ba ba, repeated softly when in contemplative play with an object or loudly in exciting games with her parents.

These repetitive, rhythmic vocalizations usually occur when the baby is in a settled state and with a familiar adult who knows the rules of the game. Increasing control over articulation means toddlers will play with intonation and sounds, whispering and making engine noises, for example.

As language emerges, toddlers not only invent words of their own for particular objects but also create chants from sounds and words, especially as they accompany movement. They play with nonsense words and create adjectives from nouns. They also play with the structure of language by building up and breaking down sentences and experimenting with different modes of speech such as questions or lists. Each of these linguistic games are detailed by Ruth Weir in her account of the pre-sleep monologues of her 2-year-old son (Weir 1962). A little of this was heard in the observation of Raj.

Meek (1985) states that alongside the urge to be understood grows the enjoyment of nonsense, rhythm, rhyme and making jokes.

> An example of this is Ryan (23 months). His mother reported, 'Ryan runs to me saying, "Poo-poo nammy, poo-poo nammy" He cannot pronounce 'p's yet. I duly start to change his nappy. As soon as I get one side undone, Ryan shrieks with laughter and says, "Jus wee-wee!" '

Meek cites this play with language as evidence of even very young children's creativity and imagination. Moreover she states, 'In a period when powerful voices are calling for a movement "back to basics" . . . respect for human imagination is one of those basics' (Meek 1985: 41).

The adult's role in supporting the communication and talk of children from birth to three

As we identified earlier, babies and toddlers have limited language and adults working with this age group need to be natural conversationalists, not put off by the lack of verbal response when playing together. Moreover, as Barrett-Pugh (in Abbott and Moylett

1997) reminds us, they must be able to provide just the right amount of what Wood *et al.* (1976) refers to as 'scaffolding' to maintain and expand the conversation or to move in their 'zone of proximal development' (Vygotsky 1978). Skilled practitioners provide a running commentary on a play scenario and use open-ended questions that encourage children to respond in ways appropriate for their age, without the need for a right answer.

Knowledge of the individual child

In addition to having knowledge and understanding of the developmental sequences of language acquisition to underpin and evaluate their practice, practitioners need to be tuned into the idiosyncrasies of individual children's speech. They also need an understanding of their role as play partners and guides and of appropriate play experiences.

We have established that in the first three years children's language is still emerging but that even a very young baby is capable of a great deal of non-verbal communication. If this is to be understood, however, the practitioner will need considerable knowledge of the individual child. This depth of knowledge contributes to the

Skilled practitioners use open-ended questions that encourage children to respond without the need for a right answer.

quality and enjoyment of their play together and reduces times of frustration and tears because a toddler cannot make the adult understand.

Naturally practitioners will never have the in-depth knowledge of the parent/carer. Equally, nor will the parent/carer understand every reference the child makes to the daycare setting. However, by working closely together each will be able to learn as much as they can from the other. For example, the information shared between Lydia's mother and Ruth, the child minder, enabled Ruth to empathize with Lydia and enriched their play together. Ruth knew what had happened on the ferry on the family's holiday, and she understood and responded appropriately to Lydia's wariness of machines as she knew her generic term for them.

Gillen (in Abbott and Moylett 1997) highlights the significance of repetition and routine in the speech and play of 2-year-olds, which she identified from listening to her own child. The observation of Lydia and her child minder gives us an insight into these common features of 2-year-olds' dialogues. First they love repeating the same song, story, game or video over and over again, without seeming to tire of it. Two-year-olds often create their own versions of these favourites. For example, Lydia when singing alone sings 'Zacchaeus was a widdle widdle man' even though she can say 'very little' and sings the correct words in church.

Another common feature is how certain words or events can trigger a 2-year-old's recall of something that may have taken place months ago. Children appear to want to have the same conversation about this event each time they recall it. They seem reassured by being able to play over what happened with someone who knows what to say. Lydia, in our observation, recalled her mother being sick three months after the event and each time would always add that she is better now. Gillen describes this as a type of mantra (in Abbott and Moylett 1997) for which there is not always an obvious trigger.

Two-year-olds (and younger) also make up their own names for things that have not come from any adult reference and apply them generally. When playing with those who know them well they can use that name in their telegraphic speech, confident that they will be understood. Lydia's 'wadawada on' can mean 'The washing machine is on' or 'Is the washing machine going to make that loud noise?' or 'I can hear a machine and it's scary.'

Practitioners playing with young children will be able to engage meaningfully in these types of dialogue by being empathetic listeners who can be trusted to be patient and not to laugh at mistakes. Young children, though skilled language learners are not yet accomplished linguists and are best helped by those tuned into their particular way of speaking. Then play will flow, the practitioner will be able to enter into the thinking and imagination of the child and they will have the privilege of being both a play partner and a facilitator.

Supporting children learning more than one language

Many children grow up in bi- or multilingual families and so are learning more than one language from birth. This has been found to advantage cognitive development; bi- or multilingual children become aware of the abstract nature of language much earlier than monolinguists (Siraj-Blatchford and Clarke 2000)

The support of mother tongue speakers and a knowledge and some understanding of each child's cultural and linguistic background in the daycare setting is essential if practitioners are going to give bi- or multilingual children an equal level of support and encouragement to that which they give to the monolingual child. If we reflect on a very young baby's sensitivity to and preference for their home language, we can better understand the significant impact on babies' and toddlers' linguistic development and on their self-esteem if they have home language speakers to play with them in the daycare setting.

An Australian project deliberately recruited early years practitioners in daycare centres and family daycare support services, who could speak the predominant languages of their multicultural community. The project had such a positive effect that a video was made of their work in order to educate and encourage other early years practitioners. The video shows babies sung to in their home language, toddlers and older children sharing the different words they have at home for the fruit they are eating and children playing ring games in each others' language (FKA 1997).

Tiny babies are in as much need of mother tongue support as 1 to 2-year-olds who are beginning to talk. An absence of someone who speaks a baby's home language does not mean a nursery cannot support that baby. A good example of this can be found in Selleck and Griffin's account of how an Italian nursery met the needs of a Chinese baby who was too distressed to play or relate to the care-givers. Daycare practitioners enlisted the parents' help to enable them to imitate the way the parents carried the baby and the rhythm and intonation patterns of the parents' language. The practitioners also asked the baby's father to record the lullabies he sang and they played this tape of the father's voice singing lullabies in the nursery. All this had a very soothing effect on a baby who had been finding it hard to adjust to the daycare setting (Selleck and Griffin in Pugh 1996).

Play experiences that support communicative children from birth to three

Practitioners – the most important play resource

The most important resource for very young children who are learning how to communicate is their close caregivers. The trusting relationships practitioners form with young children foster their confidence and self-esteem. Confident talkers take risks, express their feelings, share their ideas, dare to guess, and are less anxious about getting things wrong. In group care situations, this means having a key person system to ensure that this level of intimacy is possible. Skilled and imaginative practitioners working with children from birth to three also create rich language environments and play experiences.

The dialogue game

Protoconversations and play can be achieved through the 'dialogue game' (Barnard and Meldis 2000: 7). This is similar to imitation play but with an interesting extension. It involves the carer listening to the baby's vocalizations and picking out a particular sound, repeating back to the baby, smiling and waiting for a response. Soon the baby will repeat that sound or choose another to be echoed; the sounds can even be turned into a song. This game is then extended by taping these 'conversations' or 'songs', stating the date and name of the child at the beginning of the tape. These make interesting listening for the baby, for practitioners monitoring children's language development and particularly for the parents.

Lively language play

Between 6 and 12 months babies enjoy livelier communication games, for example, listening to the carer perform songs, dances and beat rhythms. They enjoy being moved in time to the music. Trevarthan describes these activities, 'Excite the interest and emotions of the infant, who watches eagerly, anticipates with "dread" and laughs with joy at appropriate places' (1995, in Woodhead *et al.* 1998: 92).

By 6 months old infants are able to perceive what the carer's attention is drawn to and begin to be able to follow the line of a carer's pointing (Trevarthan 1995). This enables the practitioner to draw the baby's attention to interesting sights, to indicate the names of the objects they are looking at together and, as the baby reaches and gradually points to objects, to verbalize the baby's perceived intention. For example, on seeing a baby waving their arm in the direction of a mobile a practitioner may say, 'Yes that's the dolphin mobile, oh you want to touch it do you?' and then lift them up so they can reach it.

By this age babies enjoy gentle comical teasing games. If using the previous example, the play would proceed with the carer moving so the baby can't reach any more then moving back again accompanied by suitable playful talk. This type of play teasing is only appropriate while the baby is communicating their enjoyment of the 'joke' and never beyond this or the developing trust will be damaged.

There are lots of opportunities for language play alongside the more lively play, with words to describe actions, movement and positions.

Katrina was holding Erin (8 months) high above her head and then, lowering her down to the ground. 'Up up up you pop.' she said her voice getting higher and higher, 'Down down down you drop', her voice getting deeper and gruffer. Erin responded with screams of delight. Each time she stopped Erin made up signs with both arms to communicate her desire for more.

Trevarthan (1995) states that the joy and excitement shown in such play with a trusted adult may turn to expressions of distress and fear if initiated by a stranger. It is important to strike a balance when playing with babies, as this is the age of enjoyment of the familiar and the onset of stranger anxiety.

Symbolic play

In the second year of life pretend play emerges, showing a child's ability to use symbols and therefore understand that words can be used to represent something. As this is a time of assertion of independence and practising saying no, practitioners may find their attempts to join in the play of an 18-month-old, who is feeding teddy, will be rebuffed. However the adult role is still important as they play alongside modelling and describing their own actions or giving a running commentary, for example, on what the toddler is doing and the teddy may be feeling, as well as supplying suitable real objects as play props.

Books and stories for babies and toddlers

Books, rhymes and songs are widely accepted as play experiences that promote young children's language development. However, as we stress throughout this book, it is how these are presented that is important. This is in terms of the role the adult takes and also the detail of how the book area is organized. Because of young children's limited dexterity they will be more likely to use books if they can see the front covers. It is also worth considering whether they can put the book back without damaging it and whether there is sufficient space for the children to manoeuvre around each other.

There are hundreds of excellent books for babies and toddlers. Even very young children can enjoy and be helped to handle real books; the temptation to only supply babies with board books is a false economy. Cloth or plastic bath books are not real books and do not behave as paper books do so they do not help children learn about handling and using books.

Babies and toddlers will show more interest in books that match their experiences and interests. Therefore a picture book about guinea pigs after they have met a guinea pig is ideal. Babies' and toddlers' love of repetition means that books with repetitive refrains in which they can join are very popular. One 10-month-old loved to supply the 'oh, ohs' in *We're Going on a Bear Hunt* (Rosen and Oxenbury 1989). Young children's love of rhythm and nonsense words are all included in this book and many others. Books like *Brown Bear, Brown Bear* (Carle 1984) enable children to enjoy both the rhyme and a sense of anticipation of what is coming next. Practitioners have to be prepared to read the same book over and over again.

When choosing books for babies it is as important to look out for the hidden messages they may convey as when buying books for older children. Books in which there are strong girls, gentle boys and children with disabilities in active roles will offer alternatives to the stereotypical roles portrayed elsewhere.

Two-year-olds enjoy stories that adults make up. These can specifically relate to events or situations in a child's life or may be stories that are special to the adult's life (see for example Gussin-Paley 2001). The use of real objects as story props or laminated cut-out characters (such as those Lydia was playing with) can be used. This not only promotes language development but also fosters children's creativity.

Babies and toddlers will show more interest in books that match their experiences and interests.

Left to their own devices after the story, a 2-year-old may create their own story with the props. Small photo albums with photos donated by children's families and those taken in the nursery enrich the selection and make it more personal and therefore more interesting. Taped songs and stories made by children's parents/carers in home languages and accents and a sturdy children's tape recorder can be used too.

Outings and visitors

In the nursery, little outings can be planned for small groups of toddlers. If the group is small there will be opportunity, time and attention for dialogue. Visiting interesting places or having interesting people (and animals) visit the nursery enthuses and motivates young children to want to communicate in whatever way they can. This can be extended with photographs displayed at toddler eye level, and using small photo albums. Going on local walks as described in Chapter 3 also prompts lots of rich language use.

If we look back at the observation of Lydia we can see that both planned and spontaneous play can provide rich communication and language opportunities. Ruth provided new vocabulary, used gestures to reinforce meaning, put Lydia's actions into words, verbalized Lydia's emotions and gave her explanations. Ruth's attentive presence enabled Lydia to stay focused on the play and to solve problems. Ruth also supported Lydia's sense of self through reinforcing the links between Lydia's experiences in Ruth's home and what Lydia did with her family. Moreover, the play was matched to the characteristics of the toddler in that it was unrestricted, allowing for lots of movement and fostering Lydia's independence.

6

CHILDREN FROM BIRTH TO THREE PLAYING, GROWING AND LEARNING THROUGH EXPLORING, THINKING AND IMAGINING

Understanding the context for exploratory and imaginative play

> Sarah (9 months) is seated at the Treasure Basket (Goldschmied and Jackson 1994). She leans forward to take hold of a piece of loofah, she brings it to her mouth, sucks and grimaces in a displeased way, and her whole body shivers. She puts the loofah down and lifts a shiny shell out of the basket. She drops the shell, looks down and moves her fingers across its smooth surface; she grasps hold of it and lifts it to her mouth. She pokes out her tongue and licks the shell, supporting it with her right hand to explore it with her mouth. She drops it into her lap and looks up at the practitioner, who smiles. A piece of shiny paper catches her eye and she moves her whole upper body to lean forward to reach it. She holds it up to her face. As she squeezes the paper with her hand it makes a scrunching noise.
>
> (Manning-Morton and Thorp 2001)

Exploring

In this observation of Sarah at play we can see the drive to explore the world that babies and young children possess. Like a sponge, she seems to eagerly soak up all the new experiences that the Treasure Basket offers her. All a baby's senses (of sight, smell, hearing, taste, touch and movement) are alert and are used to find out about objects and people. They explore their environment with their whole body, hands, feet, skin and especially their mouths.

Piaget (1952) described how babies build on their reflex actions through active exploration of and interaction with their own bodies and the people and objects around them. As babies move and play, they experience movement, sound, texture, light and pattern, tastes and smells. These sensory-motor experiences become mental operations called schemas. Schemas become more complex as the child assimilates experiences into their existing schemas and also adjusts their existing schemas to accommodate new experiences. In this way the child is adapting to the environment in order to maintain a state of equilibrium, a state that is always changing as the child adapts and learns from applying what they already know in different situations.

For Piaget, these early schemas are about the senses and movement and are dependent on sensory and physical interaction with the world. He proposed that the ability to form mental representations, which are separate from immediate interaction and which a baby uses to think *about* the world, only emerges at the end of the sensory-motor period (Piaget and Inhelder 1969).

Thinking

In our observation of Sarah we can see how she is processing sensory information and practising her physical skills. Her ability to find out about things does seem to be constrained by her physical abilities to sit, lean forward, reach and grasp as she plays. However current ideas arising from cognitive science suggest that babies not only take in information but also transform and rearrange it to form representations that enable them to interpret their experience and make predictions about events (Gopnik *et al*. 1999).

As babies and toddlers interact with their environment in their play, whether by swiping at a mobile, crawling after the cat or pushing a buggy around the garden, they are certainly exercising their muscles and experiencing new sensations, but they are also cognitively active, thinking about cause and effect, about relative speed and distance and about spatial relationships and the manoeuvrability of solid objects. They are also remembering past actions and experiences and recreating them, using their previous experience to plan their actions or to predict their outcome. Recent research shows that surprisingly young babies have active cognitive lives. Newborn babies recognize voices and music heard in the womb, which demonstrates learning and memory, and the first step towards abstract thought is shown when a baby shows an understanding of cause and effect by pausing and anticipating a response to their cries (Goswami 1998).

As babies play, they are processing sensory information and also thinking about and making sense of their experiences.

The evidence that infants are able to understand aspects of cause and effect and object permanence as young as 4 months old, before their motor abilities are mature enough to use them to learn about these concepts, challenges Piaget's proposal that sensory-motor behaviours *become* thought (Goswami 1998). It appears that babies are already thinking *about* their experiences; play with objects and people gives them opportunities to do this.

These kinds of evidence have given rise to the view that the fundamental cognitive processes of learning, memory, perception and attention appear to be available from, or even before birth. Gopnik *et al.* (1999) describe how babies have the ability to form cognitive representations. It seems that they have innate rules that help them to interpret sensations, with the result that their cognitive representations are different to the original sensory input. For example, Meltzoff and Moore (1983) have argued that the ability of 1–3-day-old infants to imitate tongue protrusion requires representational capacity, as they view the visual input, interpret it and recreate it as an action of their own. As babies interpret experiences they form expectations and create theories about the world, which they test out in their play.

Images

In the process of transforming perceptual information into knowledge, Jean Mandler suggests that babies form representations of the spatial properties of objects and events. She says that babies select the key information about events to form 'image schemas' (Mandler 1992). For example, babies have innumerable perceptual experiences of containment, in and out of the bath, pram and adult's arms; food in and out of the bottle, bowl, mouth, stomach; clothes on and off. They recognize what is similar about the movements and spatial relations of these events and then create a containment image-schema that includes the crucial elements of containment, i.e. interior, exterior and boundary. This image-schema would be closely related to image-schemas for going in and going out. As babies mature physically we can see them exploring this particular schema in their play with great enthusiasm: dressing up in layers of clothes; turning their bowl over; dropping toys out of the cot; painting borders around their pictures; posting toys into the video player; playing peek-a-boo or reaching to be picked up and cuddled.

Representing our experiences with actions is something we continue to do through our lives. Bruner (1966) called this the enactive mode of representation. As children make their internal images explicit, they are able to represent their experiences with an external image, the iconic mode of representation (Bruner 1966). We noted in Chapter 4 how toddlers become fascinated with photographs of themselves, thereby developing an early understanding of iconic representation.

Symbols

Declarative pointing and first words are the beginning of children's symbolic behaviour; Jean Mandler (1996) suggests that image-schemas are pre-verbal representations that facilitate language acquisition. The following example illustrates the development of an image-schema of containment into language, to represent symbolically the more complex idea of containment/position/difficulty.

> At between 12 and 14 months Billie would say what sounded like 'duck'. Her parents knew that she was saying 'stuck' and that this meant either 'I can't reach what I want' (accompanied by pointing to an out of reach object) or 'I can't get it in' (when squeezing too large a cork into her posting tin) or 'I can't get out of my highchair/buggy (reaching arms up or pulling at straps).

Representations help children and adults to hold on to, or recall, things and people when they are not there and to make new connections between images, objects, events and marks (Whitehead 1996). Babies begin this through imitating the facial expressions and actions of adults and older children and making movements that mirror the shape or movement of an object. This kind of imitation is not just copying, as the child is interpreting and reconstructing the experience. For Piaget (1962) imitation and the formation of internal images are important elements of symbolic behaviour and pretend play.

In the second year of life we can see the increasing manifestation of the use of symbols. Piaget (1962) describes his daughter at 1-year-old, unintentionally falling backwards onto her pillow in her cot. She then put herself into her usual position for sleeping but smiling to herself, then she sat up delighted with her 'make believe'. She repeated this play several times during the day when not in her cot and without the pillow, clearly using symbolic representation, making her actions stand for the act of sleeping. For Piaget (1962) symbolism arises from the progressive abstraction of actions from everyday rituals and we can see this in the way that toddlers often re-enact familiar scenarios in their play such as 'being' a baby, or feeding and cuddling a 'baby' in their play. Toddlers use everyday objects in apparent rehearsal of future roles, such as talking on the telephone. In this scenario their imaginative actions are guided by the properties of the object, which Vygotsky (1966) would say is not true symbolic, pretend play, as the representation is not separated completely from the object. However toddlers also use different objects to stand for familiar items, such as blocks for telephones or hairbrushes. They may also use their transitional object to stand for themselves in a game (Bruce 1997).

Babies and toddlers often use personal symbols, developing their own signs and gestures (Acredolo and Goodwyn 2000) and words for things. At the same time they begin to use culturally specific symbols, such as waving good-bye or kissing on both cheeks. Bruner (1966) suggests that in this process a child is initiated into their culture.

Social and emotional contexts

Our increased understanding of the complexity of babies' and toddlers' cognitive development may lead us to see them solely as little scientists carrying out their research on the world and to think we only have to provide special brain-enriching play activities for them to develop fully. Certainly toddlers are always investigating and wanting hands-on experience and proof of what they are told and what they see but we have to remember that their intellectual investigations take place within a social and emotional context.

Being part of a social network of other people is a crucial aspect of cognitive development (Gopnik *et al.* 1999). Engaging in play behaviours such as mutual imitation, and involving babies and toddlers in the everyday real tasks of the home or nursery enables them to learn in just the way they need, playing in contexts of social and emotional meaning.

> Sam was tearing lettuces for lunch in half an hour's time. This was not only refining his fine motor skills but was also supporting his sense of belonging as he was able to contribute to his group's mealtime. This activity therefore, carried much more meaning for him than tearing paper for sticking onto a picture relating to the adult's chosen theme.

For babies and toddlers the majority of their experiences are new and strange which may be interesting and exciting but can also be scary and overwhelming. The rapid changes in intellectual growth in the first three years of life can cause toddlers to alter their perspective on things constantly. If two things happen simultaneously, or if two things have some similar characteristics (although we may know they are totally unconnected) the toddler may link them in their mind. This can lead them to develop fears that to adults are inexplicable and irrational. For example:

> Luke developed a fear of the vacuum cleaner for no obvious reason. But a vacuum cleaner hose may swallow dirt on the carpet like the snake in a familiar storybook swallowed other animals. It is only a small jump for Luke at 2 years old to imagine it swallowing him.

As we know from dealing with our own fears (spiders, heights, etc.), someone forcing us to confront our fear or dismissing it does not make a fear go away. Empathy and gradual exposure to what is feared that the child (or frightened adult) can control, is by far the most helpful and respectful way.

The high level of new, unpredictable and incomprehensible experiences in a toddler's life means that sometimes they need certain things to stay the same. They develop rituals over which they can have some control. For example:

Carys insists on using the same colour cup at lunchtime and Sacha always needs to hear the 'Goodnight' song at rest time. They can get very distressed if these predictable and understandable routines change for reasons they cannot grasp.

Practitioners who honour individual children's rituals and provide just the right amount of structure and routine in the day help the toddler to feel confident and secure.

Dispositions

Babies and toddlers respond to play experiences in individual ways. Some seem to have a go at everything; others may hang back and approach new things with caution. For some children these approaches vary according to the situation, for others it seems to be a more consistent approach to life. Attention to the social and emotional contexts of children's play is crucial as they are not only learning particular skills and knowledge, but also acquiring dispositions through the way play experiences are presented by the adult.

A disposition is a tendency to frequently exhibit a pattern of behaviour or a habit of mind, a tendency to respond to situations in certain ways (Katz 1988). Dispositions such as friendliness or wariness are learned, primarily through the interactions and responses of people who are important to the child but also though the kinds of play situations the child experiences.

Some dispositions such as curiosity are thought to be innate, providing young children with a drive to find out about the world and underpinning their exploratory play. However, curiosity, like any other disposition, can be strengthened or weakened according to the responses of the adults and the nature of the environment (Katz 1988). In this way the development of dispositions to play and learning are closely related to children's self-concept and emotional well-being (Laevers *et al.* 1997).

Involvement

Katz (1988) suggests that the assessment of children's level of curiosity and interest are important indicators of their dispositions to learning. It is not sufficient, however, to assess children's development without also evaluating the provision for their play.

The nature of the environment and materials offered can strengthen or weaken positive dispositions such as curiosity.

Ferre Laevers (1994) has developed the Leuven Involvement Scale (LIS) as a means of assessing the effects of the learning situation on the child, by observing and rating the child's level of involvement in play according to certain defined signals. He describes involvement as a quality of human activity that can be recognized by concentration and persistence. It is characterized by motivation and fascination, openness to stimuli and intensity of experience both at the sensory and cognitive level. When children show a high level of involvement there is deep satisfaction and a strong flow of energy at the bodily and spiritual level. Activities that possess a fair amount of the quality of 'involvement' enhance children's development (Laevers 1994: 5).

When using the LIS in settings for children from birth to three, care needs to be taken when interpreting the defined signals. For example the signal of 'concentration' would need to be interpreted in the context of toddlers' interest in being mobile. Babies and toddlers are often deeply involved in exploring when they are moving about, such as we saw in the observation of Raj in Chapter 3; sitting still does not necessarily mean that they are concentrating.

However, many of the 'signals of involvement' used to measure children's interest are relevant to children from birth to three, especially those of 'energy' and 'facial expression and posture'. An evaluative framework that assesses how the adults are providing for children in a way that supports children's play is a useful tool in developing good quality play for children from birth to three.

Playing and thinking ██

Schemas

> Nena is observed to repeat and practise a containment schema. She puts the large wooden pegs in and out of the holes in the activity car whenever it is available. Sometimes she does it with her left hand and from a different angle, thereby extending the level of difficulty for herself and sometimes she repeats the action in its simplest form, which does not require her full attention. Then she struggles with the more complex task of fitting the shapes into the posting box. She puts cups, bowls and tubs in and out of each other and the home corner oven. She is fascinated by the large equipment going in the shed and enjoys helping with this task and others such as putting toys into boxes and tissues in bins. She plays peek-a-boo in three different ways, by peering around others, by covering herself with a cloth and by putting her hands over her face. Nena is very aware of practitioners going in and out of the room and, when anxious, puts her thumb in her mouth and asks to be in her key person's arms.

Athey (1990) used a Piagetian framework of schematic thought to observe patterns in children's thoughts and behaviour in play. Her development of the idea of schemas as both mental structures and as patterns of behaviour reflects how the biological development of the brain is in constant interaction with the child's sociocultural experiences (Bruce 1997).

Athey (1990) encourages practitioners to focus on the form rather than the content of children's play. In so doing it may be seen that children who appear to be flitting from one activity to another, may in fact be exploring a particular idea or concept in some depth. As they move around exploring their ideas, babies and toddlers can be observed to be frequently exploring a particular pattern of thought and movement such as in and out, transporting or rotation, exhibiting an underlying logic in their play such as we see in the observation above.

Play that appears idiosyncratic or even mischievous can also give clues to children's schematic preoccupations. Pouring sand from the sand tray to the floor or watching the juice trickle down from the upturned feeder cup onto the table top and then over the edge onto the floor may be born of an interest in vertical trajectories rather than a deliberate attempt to annoy the adult. Understanding this does not mean condoning antisocial behaviour but allows the practitioner to provide for the child appropriately, such as supplying another tray or wide container on the floor to pour the sand into. The adult's observation of the form enables them to feed the content of play, thus extending and enriching the child's experience.

Bruce (1997) describes schemas as functioning at different levels in early childhood. Children use schemas at a sensory-motor level, through their senses, actions and movements. Matthews (1994: 41) observed his son Joel exploring arcing trajectories at this level. He was 13 months old at the time.

> Joel likes to carry his cup of milk around with him. However, co-ordinating these two new skills is not easy and he frequently spills milk. On one occasion, the milk falls on to a smooth, shiny concrete floor. Joel, his jaw dropping, watches with great interest the spreading shape. Then, he puts his right hand into the milk and starts to smear it, using the horizontal arching motion. He quickly brings his other hand into play, so that both hands are fanning to and fro in synchrony, meeting in the midline, until they become out of phase. In this way, he makes the two sectors of a circle in the spilt milk.

Soon after this his father introduced him to paint and Joel is able to explore this schema further with the new medium.

When the sensory-motor level is well established, children (and adults) will also use their schemas at a symbolic level, when they make something stand for something else, and at a cause and effect level, when they make something happen as a result of what they do. Children from birth to three manifest their schemas dynamically through movements and actions such as dancing round, climbing up or crawling into and configuratively through painting or modelling.

This way of understanding children's play encourages practitioners to closely observe babies' and toddlers' play and to take their lead from what the children are showing interest in. Drawing parents/ carers into observing schemas can lead to them feeling very involved in their child's learning. This is easy to do when children manifest their schemas configuratively in their drawings, paintings and models; however these should not be valued more highly than the dynamic aspect, which would need to be recorded in written or video observations or in photographs to share effectively. As Tina Bruce (1997: 65) says, 'the study of schemas . . . helps adults to understand children better . . . to relate to children more easily and to enjoy their company more, as well as helping the children to learn in deep and thorough ways'.

However, not all children at all times show one or two strong schemas and we must be careful not to reduce the range of play opportunities we are offering because we have overinterpreted very young children's natural exploratory behaviour from too little evidence. A once-observed lining up of crayons across the table is not confirmation of a deep interest in horizontal trajectories. As Bruce (1997: 67) states, the study of schemas is not a curriculum nor should it 'be viewed in isolation from other aspects of a child's development and learning, but within the context of traditional good nursery practice'.

Explorative and creative play

> Emmett (16 months) stacked the tins three high, then carefully placed a cardboard tube in the top tin – the whole thing toppled. Three times he repeated this, each time with the same result. The fourth time Emmett put some chains in the top tin and paused – the stack stayed up. He continued to experiment with stacking and filling for 15 minutes. All the time his key person was quietly seated a metre away, watching with interest, and occasionally scooping a few more resources into Emmett's reach. She went on to make a discovery area of these Heuristic Play materials on low shelves, so it would be accessible all week – maybe for longer.

Hutt (1989) defines play as in three categories: epistemic, ludic and games with rules. In her research she observed how children engage in first epistemic then ludic play when encountering a new object. In epistemic play children gain knowledge through exploring and prob-lem-solving play, to see what things do and how they work. They then incorporate these ideas into their imaginative, ludic play, which is repetitive and lacks a specific focus; this is play for sheer entertain-ment. She viewed all three categories as valuable, but described 'epistemic play' as more likely to aid cognitive development, whereas ludic play brings enjoyment and mastery of skills (Hutt 1989).

With this kind of differentiation practitioners may be tempted to value epistemic play more highly, adopting a 'play as work' approach. It might be that we find the gains children make in epistemic play easier to define, whereas the development of creative expression arising from ludic play may be harder to measure. Yet we know that the creative expression of our inner thoughts and feelings is an essential aspect of our being and is a crucial contribution to society as a whole. The challenge to practitioners is to provide challenging materials and opportunities for epistemic play, which continue to be available in order for ludic play to develop from this. Interesting new materials only brought out occasionally will not allow young children to progress from discovering what they can do with them to incorporating them into their imaginative play.

> Imagination can be taught ... (or crushed) bringing out the children's creativity – recognising it and fostering it is important. Creativity and imagination are not gifts just a few have. We want children's pockets to be full of creativity and imagination.
>
> (Gambetti 2000)

Free flow play

Tina Bruce (1991) places a very high value on children having the opportunity to engage in 'free flow play'. She states that children learn about ideas, relationships, and their bodies as well as the spiritual and moral self through play. She acknowledges that while

Interesting new materials need to continue to be available to be incorporated into imaginative play.

play is not the only way children learn, play has a central role as it integrates and helps children make sense of everything they learn (Bruce 1991). She defines 12 features of free flow play, many of which relate closely to the play of children from birth to three. Certainly the emphasis on the active process of play rather than the product and the intrinsic motivation of children's play are central to the play we observe in babies and toddlers.

Bruce (1997) emphasizes that the role of the early years practitioner is to ensure that there is sufficient time, choice and space for children to have quality play experiences. In this way they can support the 'wallowing in ideas, feelings and relationships plus the application of developed competence, mastery and control' that combine to become free flow play (Bruce 1991: 60).

Those working and living with under-3s can probably give many examples of children learning about ideas, relationships, and their bodies through play. Time, space and sufficient, appropriate choice for free flow play is one of the most important aspects of providing quality play experiences for children under 3.

The role of the adult in supporting the explorative and creative play of children from birth to three

Observing play

As in all other aspects of play, a fundamental aspect of the practitioner's role in supporting explorative and creative play is to carefully observe their key children's use of the materials provided and plan further activities that allow them to practise skills and explore their ideas in different ways. In this way the play experiences that are provided are more likely to be meaningful to that particular group of children, matched to their abilities and focused on what they can do or nearly do with support. However the practitioners' observations cannot stand alone or the context of children's experience will be lost. All the adults involved with a child need to be able to share information about the child's current interests and preoccupations in order to better understand their play.

Practitioners' involvement in play

When caregivers have fun and take delight in reciprocal play, children experience the joy of being human.

(Greenman and Stonehouse 1996: 254)

Sitting in the spacious home corner, Rachel is playing alongside a small group of 2–3-year-old children as they move in and out of the area. During their play together she wonders with Joshua, Isaiah and Adenola why the oven door will not shut with the bowl inside and mediates between Oliver and Isaiah for use of the oven glove. She models and reflects the children's imaginative scenarios; 'Ooh its warming up,' she says as the oven is 'turned on' and she 'eats' 'ice and cheese' offered to her on a plate. She follows the children's lead as Anna asks to phone her mummy and encourages the other children to find another phone so they can each 'phone' their mummies. When imagining talking to their mummies, she encourages pretend play and supports language by emphasizing key words and by using sign and gesture, especially for the children learning English as an additional language. The words she emphasizes are those she knows are of particular interest to the children such as 'Tweenies', 'car' and 'lion'.

(Key Times Video 2001)

The practitioner is the most important piece of play equipment in a setting. Therefore being involved with children during play is an essential part of their role. To do this, practitioners need to place themselves at the child's level, which with babies and toddlers is most often on the floor. Younger babies are less able to amuse themselves so it is important that practitioners make themselves available for extended periods of time. Playing alongside the children enables the practitioner to use opportune moments to sensitively expand the children's play by suggesting new ideas or adding new props to their play areas, without needlessly interrupting the children's play.

A practitioner who has in-depth knowledge of where a child is developmentally can build on their skills and knowledge in the context of their play and engage in and extend the imaginative content of their play. Being a play partner means following the children's lead and what they are interested in even though it may be different to the planned activity. Supporting free flow play entails practitioners being flexible, encouraging babies and toddlers to explore and experiment with materials in their own ways and using minimum direction. With babies it is important not to overwhelm them with your own activity so the practitioner needs to adapt their behaviour to the babies' cues. Practitioners need to be sensitive to when or whether their involvement in the children's play is what is required at any one time and to balance supporting or scaffolding children's play with allowing their autonomous exploration and expression.

Praise

Adults working and living with children from birth to three are aware of how much young children are keen to please their significant adults and we often praise their behaviours to let them know that we are pleased. However the use of indiscriminate praise, such as 'good boy', does not let a child know what it is they have done that is 'good' and comments such as 'you're playing nicely' are obscure and make a judgement about what 'playing nicely' is. Neither comment is helpful to the child developing inner understanding and control of themselves.

In the same way, praise that only focuses on the child's products or achievements, such as 'well done' does not sufficiently acknowledge the efforts that a child has made. This results in learned helplessness, where a child believes that what they do is only worthwhile if approved of by an adult, and so stops relying on their own judgement and intrinsic satisfaction with their activities (Katz 1988).

> A practitioner sitting near the painting area noticed that when she said, 'What a lovely picture', to one child who brought their painting to her, another quickly went to the easel, daubed a few quick lines with the brush and brought the finished product to her for approval.

This does not mean we should not appreciate children's achievements but we should also empathize with their frustrations, acknowledging their efforts, not just their successes. Adults need to share in the children's delight at their discoveries and their mastery, showing genuine interest and enthusiasm. If young children sense that a practitioner's response is not authentic they will lose trust in them.

Supporting creativity

John Matthews says that skills in the use of actions, shapes and objects to build unique forms, to represent experiences, objects and events, or to express emotion, emerge in an arena formed between infant and caregiver; a space which is both physical and psychological. Without these skills, any fluent use of representational media, or of symbols and signs, would not be possible (Matthews 1999).

Understanding this, the effective practitioner will be very aware of their influence on a child's developing creativity, which permeates their play and learning. Babies and toddlers are interested in natural phenomena such as dust in sunbeams, watching their shadows follow them and the moon in the afternoon sky; this means being outside with babies and toddlers, supporting their fascination with the natural world.

Babies and toddlers respond to different types of music and song by moving their whole body and making sounds with their own voices and with objects; they also choose to engage in movement for its own sake and use it expressively. In the young child it may be seen in the waving, beating and shaking of arms, and in slightly older children the equally spontaneous activities of gliding, leaping, whirling, swirling and fluttering (Davies 1995/2002). Babies and toddlers use the movement of their whole bodies to recreate or represent an experience, such as spinning around on one leg after playing on a roundabout.

We describe babies' and toddlers' creative play with language in Chapter 5 and the importance of nurturing young children's play with language and the development of narrative is of great interest to practitioners keen to support early literacy. Vivian Gussin-Paley has written extensively about the importance of the imaginative development of stories for the social and personal understanding of 4–7-year-olds. In her book *In Mrs Tulley's Room* (2001) she describes how her approach to listening to children's stories and acting them out can also be used with 2-year-olds. Their story scripts are one, two or three words long: 'Mama', 'Mommy, wipe up' and 'Tuck me in, Baby', and the subject matter mostly about their mothers, as if their purpose is to keep their mothers in mind. She comments that the 2-year-olds 'are *doing* stories' (2001: 5) as they each interpret the word 'Mama' with a different action or movement and she describes how they use each other as part of their dramatization.

> Mrs Tulley says, returning to the bench. 'It's a mystery, don't you think? I mean the way these babies take to story telling it's like they were born doing it.' Funny thing, most folks I meet at conferences don't even know the twos can do it. Even though it's nothing different than play.
>
> (Gussin-Paley 2001: 7)

The types of creative play discussed above are not always noticed or provided for in settings for children from birth to three. Painting and drawing are more commonly provided as creative activities. However, this does not necessarily mean that children's creativity is being adequately supported, especially when fostering children's creativity is thought to equate with the reproducing of an adult's idea of, for example, a daffodil, and when babies' and toddlers' own spontaneous creations are not seen as important, as they do not look like anything the adults recognize.

Understanding the process of how babies and toddlers become skilled, imaginative painters and drawers can help practitioners resist pressure from parents and colleagues to produce an end product. Young children's imagination and creativity is not supported by painting on a shape or object drawn by an adult, or colouring in photocopied sheets. Frieze making may turn painting and drawing activities into meaningless tasks more appropriate for preparing someone to work on factory assembly lines than to be an inventive cook or designer. Toddlers may be deterred from playing with painting activities if aprons are insisted on or if they can only join in if they sit down at the table, especially if art activities always involve a lot of waiting and turn-taking.

Effective practitioners value a child's pictorial representations by treating them respectfully. For example, by mounting and displaying them with care and not cutting paintings or drawings into a different shape or writing over them. They also understand that children often describe their pictures in relation to the nature of the actions they used to create it, and so are attentive to a child's creative explorations, providing assistance in a way that does not disrupt the child's flow of thinking and through their unobtrusive support, giving the child the emotional security to experiment.

In all, effective practitioners understand that babies and toddlers acquire new skills and understanding through play, exploration and daily life experiences. They value and encourage play as integral to children's daily experiences and see education as inseparable to good care. They value their professional roles as both carers and educators of young children and understand that teaching young children means being a facilitator, a role model, an observer, and a 'scaffolder' of children's learning rather than being an instructor.

Play experiences for exploring, thinking and imagining birth to three-year-olds ■

The appropriateness of play experiences offered to children from birth to three can be judged by the degree to which they match individual children's development and interests and to how finely tuned they are to the characteristics of babies and toddlers. The

Effective practitioners are facilitators and partners in children's play.

Treasure Basket and Heuristic Play (Goldschmied and Jackson 1994) are examples of two play experiences with a high degree of match to the development of sitting but non-mobile babies and of toddlers of 12 to 20 months respectively. They are designed to meet the children's strong desire to explore in their characteristic ways.

Exploring the treasure basket

Elinor Goldschmied devised the Treasure Basket for babies like Sarah, who can sit independently and therefore are in an ideal position to explore. She states it should be filled with objects that are made of natural materials, the sort of things in everyday use in the home, thus providing rich sensory play experiences of differing textures, temperatures, weight, shape, sounds and tastes. She recommends that babies should be seated with support if needed, sideways to the basket to facilitate ease of exploration. The basket should have straight sides so it can be leant on without tipping over. The adult is advised to remain quiet but attentive and resist the urge to participate as the babies play, providing a secure base and allowing the babies to explore at their own pace (Goldschmied and Jackson 1994).

Exploring and investigating in heuristic play

Heuristic Play, like the Treasure Basket, provides a wealth of materials for exploration and is tuned to the characteristics of a toddler, such as being physically active and enjoying collecting, distributing, emptying and refilling, shaking, banging and investigating. The different containers and the various objects that can be collected and transported are set out for the toddlers to explore in a specially prepared area for defined play periods (Goldschmied and Jackson 1994).

The large number of each type of object and the wide variety of materials provided facilitate long periods of concentrated play with very few disputes. Heuristic Play develops children's ability to solve problems, to develop skills in perceiving differences and similarities and to make choices and experiment, as can be seen from the observation of Emmet earlier in this chapter.

Exploring and thinking through schemas

Although John plays in different places and with different materials he still seems to show a fascination with enclosing things – he covers his head with the quilt at sleep time, he wraps the soap and nail brush in paper towels, he sits in the sand pit and covers his legs with sand. On noticing this we introduced gift-wrapping paper in the art area, a basket of headscarves next to the dressing-up box and put a water play tray full of shredded paper on the floor for him to climb into.

John is seen here exploring his interest in enveloping, for another child it may be transporting. Details of common schemas observed in children from birth to three can be found in the Key Times Framework (Manning-Morton and Thorp 2001). Planning play experiences that facilitate children's thinking and exploration in this way achieves a high degree of match to an individual child's interests and thinking. Often, materials provided for one child are also used by another. For example, Freya's transforming schema led her to mix the shredded paper provided for John's enveloping schema in the wok with the sand and water.

Experimenting and imagining with mark-making materials

Babies and toddlers are often fascinated by their ability to make marks with food, drink, sticks, stones and water, as well as the more conventional drawing and painting resources (Duffy 1998). Their confidence in their own creativity, their ability to express themselves and to communicate develops as they explore and experiment with mark-making materials and tools. Again it is the degree of fit of the play experiences offered that will influence the children's concept of themselves as creative people.

Lengths of wallpaper, plain side up, covered the whole floor of the room. Five wide-bottomed powder paint buckets had been placed on the floor and a variety of brushes and rollers. Each bucket was about a quarter full of different colour paint. Elly brought Nuala (10 months), John (22 months), Liam and Freya (both 18 months) into the room just wearing nappies. John went straight to the red paint and began to dip his hands in the paint and smear it over his arms and legs. Freya took the blue paint and poured it into the yellow, and

Babies and toddlers are often fascinated about their ability to make marks.

carefully stirred the mixture. Elly was at hand to offer other things she could add to her mixture without emptying the others' buckets. Liam's love of banging meant that he soon tired of spreading arcs with his arm and went from bucket to bucket first dabbing his brush in the bucket then on the paper. Nuala watched him with interest and then began to imitate his actions.

This experience was finely tuned to the children's development. They were able to use large arm and leg movements and their whole bodies to explore paint and to make marks. It is much later that wrists and fingers are sufficiently developed to use smaller tools and surfaces. Their limbs were not restricted by clothing and tubs of water were ready in the bathroom for a water play/bathing session. The practitioners took the role of observing and facilitating the children's play and were nearby when children's interests conflicted.

Practitioners can provide a variety of mark-making experiences and different surfaces to make marks on. In addition to cornflour, paint and pens, toddlers can be given house-painting brushes and little buckets of water to use on dry pavements or walls, or a water play tray of dry lentils or flour. Mud, wet sand and puddles to pat, smear, stamp and even roll in, all make exciting mark-making experiences. If these materials are available day after day skills learnt will not be forgotten and children's painting, drawing, and creating skills will grow. In addition toddlers, being natural imitators, may learn new techniques from their peers.

Dorothy Selleck (1997: 14) recalls a scene of children playing outside after a shower of rain in a Reggio Emilia nursery.

Rustling ribbons of packaging were tucked into the back of some toddlers dungarees. They were strutting like peacocks with folded tail feathers, cooing and hooting with excitement as they trailed their tails through puddles. The wet trailing ribbons made intriguing patterns on the path. The toddlers delighted in their extensions and their pavement art . . . At the end of the activity the muddy ribbons went in the bin, the trailing wet art evaporated in the sunshine.

A key aspect of this creative experience is its close match to the toddlers' characteristic mobility. The importance of physical movement for creativity is reflected in this statement from the sculptor Barbara Hepworth, whose creativity was profoundly influenced by her early experiences:

All my early memories are of forms and shapes and textures. Moving through and over the West Riding landscape with my father in his car, the hills were sculptures; the roads defined the form. Above all, there was the sensation of moving physically over the contours of fulnesses and concavities, through hollows and over peaks – feeling, touching, seeing, through mind and hand and eye. The sensation has never left me. I, the sculptor, am the landscape.

(Barbara Hepworth Museum 1977).

The authors would echo the wish of Gambetti (2000) 'We want children's pockets to be full of imagination and creativity.'

7

CREATING ROUTINES AND ENVIRONMENTS THAT SUPPORT THE PLAY, GROWTH AND LEARNING OF CHILDREN FROM BIRTH TO THREE

Creating time for play in physical care routines

Sue and two of her key children are in the bathroom, Alex (27 months) who is in nappies, and learning to use the toilet and Paulette (30 months) an experienced toilet user. Paulette disappears into a cubicle as Sue squats down beside Alex. Sue begins the now familiar mantra:

Sue: What are we going to do? We are going to take your nappy off, then?

Sue and Alex (in unison): Alex go to the toilet! (Both look enthusiastic about this prospect.)

Sue: Shall we take your shorts off first to make it easier?

Sue pulls them down a little way. Alex does the rest; stepping out of them she hands them to Sue.

Hand in hand they go to the toilet cubicle. Alex backs in, Sue bends down and loosens one side of her nappy.

'Do you want to do it?' Sue asks. Alex pulls it off and backs on to the low-level toilet. As Sue disposes of the nappy, Alex swings the metre high door shut with her foot. She likes it 'only close, not locked'. Paulette and Alex laugh and call to each other through the cubicle wall. Paulette is in the next cubicle with the door bolted.

Sue: Do you need any help, Paulette? Have you done a wee yet? (They chat together.)

Alex: I did a wee!
Sue (smiling over the door):   You have done a wee, well done!

Soon both children are side by side at the low-level washbasins soaping, then rinsing their hands and the mirrors above with great enthusiasm.

Sue: Hey Paulette, Alex did a wee in the toilet. (Paulette has been the expert peer helping Alex learn the ropes.)
Paulette: Alex did a wee wee in the toilet!

She smiles at Alex. Alex repeats this with pride. Paulette twists the running tap off and reaches for a paper towel. She dries her hands and the mirror and posts the towel in the bin. Alex copies.

(Key Times Video 2001)

Care and play in the curriculum

The relative values of 'caring' and 'educating', where more status and legitimacy is ascribed to 'educating', poses a dilemma for practitioners. How to give appropriate emphasis to well-thought-out routines for children's physical care and yet still gain credibility for the support practitioners are giving to children's learning through play requires understanding and the ability to articulate what a broad and balanced curriculum really is for children from birth to three. As can be seen from the observation above, babies and toddlers are learning through play in the bathroom, at the meal table, in the sleep area and throughout the day.

Adopting a balanced approach means viewing the curriculum as more than a plan for play activities during non-routine times; it means giving appropriate time and thought to the whole day. Routine care times are key times for one to one interaction, for focused attention, sustained conversation and repeating and recalling experiences. They are times when favourite games can be played. Sue commented:

Paulette and Alex's mirror washing is as much a part of their bathroom routine as using the toilet. They delight in making their reflections disappear and finding them again as they soap and rinse their mirrors.

Practitioners planning such a curriculum recognize that for babies and toddlers the separation between play and physical care is as indistinct as that between play and learning activities.

Balance can be achieved when the whole day is planned and there is discussion of:

- the sensitivity and availability of the practitioners throughout the day, especially at care times;
- the way mealtimes are organized, including the time just before and after meals;
- the way the physical care times of bathroom, dressing and sleeping, are organized;
- how opportunities for play can be maximized and tuned to the interests, ability and characteristics of babies and toddlers;
- the way the day flows, the time allotted for routine care and the flexibility of the timetable;
- the attitude towards differences of gender, race, ability and differences of family form that is engendered in the group;
- the way the physical play environment is planned, including accessibility of equipment and the type of resources and furniture used;
- the provisions for settling new children and greeting children daily, helping them to say goodbye to parents and to settle into the day.

Greenman and Stonehouse's book *Prime Times* emphasizes the importance of well planned care times, describing them as 'prime times' and acknowledging that

> Designing caring routines that actually empower children and enhance their development is a huge challenge in group care . . . the major goal of the rich built in learning environment is to engage children in independent play that allows caregivers relaxed time to diaper or nurture them: to touch, to talk, to listen, to play all the call response games that children set in motion.
>
> (1996: 107–8)

Sadly these times of the day are also identified by practitioners as the most hectic and demanding, when babies' intense needs to eat or sleep are most likely to occur all at once. They are also times when the plans of the carer and those of the toddler are most likely to be at odds, especially when the child sees an opportunity to play where the practitioner does not.

When practitioners change from seeing these times as 'routine' to regarding them as 'prime times', times of important life-learning play opportunities, they give them the time and recognition they need. Paulette and Alex were learning about how to teach and encourage others, respecting other's preferences and friendship, good hygiene, physical control and care for themselves and the effect of soap and water on mirrored glass.

The practitioner's approach

Greenman and Stonehouse (1996) suggest the following general guidelines for practitioners in approaching physical care routines:

- to keep the importance of children developing a positive self-concept uppermost in their minds;
- to remember that their body language, voice tone and the way they handle children convey messages to the child;
- to avoid talking to other staff about the children as if they were not there;
- to not let their own attitudes to food, bodily waste, or dirt make a caring time negative for a child.

Practitioners may find it helpful to reflect on the degree to which care routines enable the children to play and be themselves. For toddlers that means being physically active, assertive, ritualistic, fluctuating between independence and dependence, in the here and now, needing help in self-control, having an unpredictable attention span and sudden fears, limited in communication, frequently changing their minds, imitators, busy and curious. All these are key characteristics of 1 to 3-year-olds (Stonehouse 1988).

Practitioners may also wish to reflect on how they feel by the end of each care time. Good organization can result in key workers feeling proud of their work because they have been appropriately involved and have created time and opportunity for play. They have allowed children who need to be dependent to cling to them, while allowing others the time and access to resources to be independent.

While the above are laudable aims to be included in the policies of centres providing for children from birth to three, babies and toddlers do not read these documents. They experience them through the practitioners' attention to the fine detail of interactions as illustrated in the observation at the beginning of this chapter.

Separation times

Greenman and Stonehouse (1996) suggest that the way young children and their parents separate can affect the quality of their experiences throughout the rest of the day. Parting rituals that have been worked out with each parent and that are recorded so all can follow them enable young children to feel secure, able to understand and predict what is happening and to settle down to play. If key workers are free to greet both parent and child as they arrive and are not setting up the play experiences and receiving children simultaneously, they will be more able to provide the necessary support during this transition period. Moreover, if the environment supports independent play, and does not require a high level of adult involvement, this time will be less stressful for the practitioners too.

Babies and toddlers who are upset at separation times will be reassured more readily if the key person empathizes with their distress. An enormous amount can be communicated to babies and toddlers by tone, body language and physical handling.

A baby or toddler gently held and told empathetically, 'I know, it's horrible when you have to say good bye to Daddy', is calmed more fully than the child who is jigged vigorously up and down and is told, 'Never mind, come and look at the hamster.'

There is certainly a place for offering distressed children alternative interesting things to focus on like feeding the hamster or returning to something that they were playing with just before their parent left. However, doing this without acknowledging the child's grief does not show respect for their feelings or teach the child that it is okay to be upset. Besides, distressed children cannot play while in this state.

If milestones of the day are used to explain when the parent will return it will be much more meaningful to the child than being told that their mummy will be back later.

Gina (2.6 years) was reassured by her key worker that her mummy was 'coming after sandwiches' (which is what she called teatime). The choice and control she was given over what happened to her transitional object 'doggy', also helped this same child. She usually brought it to the office after her nap and asked for it to be put on the windowsill 'to watch for mummy'. This enabled her to go off and play happily.

(Manning-Morton and Thorp 2001)

Washing, toilet and changing times

There may be more time and opportunity for play and for a toddler's independence and social skills to be fostered at washing, toilet and nappy-changing times if each key person takes their key group to the bathroom. It may feel less stressful and more enjoyable for both children and practitioners. Meanwhile, the remaining key groups can continue to play at an existing activity or may each enjoy a singing time, a story, or putting the rest beds out. The bathroom can foster children's independence if towels, bins and toilet paper are accessible and the taps are those that small fingers can turn on and off. The positive effect of these measures is apparent by the degree of confidence and autonomy shown by Alex and Paulette in the observation.

Part of getting the conditions right for play is creating an atmosphere of consideration and care between children and between adults and children. Key workers who consult babies and toddlers about their intention to change their nappy, wash their faces or wipe their noses model this behaviour. Opportunities that arise when children are comparing their physical characteristics can also be used and practitioners can acknowledge differences and similarities between children sensitively and positively. Low-level mirrors and laminated pictures of the children encourage play and discussion

For babies and toddlers there is no separation between play and routine care times.

about such things. Older toddlers, like Paulette, may take pride in passing on their expertise and toddlers' social skills and self-esteem will be supported.

Meal and snack times

There is little more important to children and adults than eating. Offering familiar foods can be of comfort to an unsettled or new child (Greenman and Stonehouse 1996). If young children are allowed to use mealtimes as a time to play and learn they will be more likely to eat and enjoy the nutritious food offered and to develop an emotionally healthy disposition towards food. Young children are interested in food and drink and want to play with and investigate the textures, colours and consistencies. They are keen to mix, tip, pour and make patterns with fingers, spoons or forks as the observation of Joel in Chapter 6 showed (Matthews 1994). Some practitioners find they have to review messages from their own upbringing in order to allow this.

A good atmosphere is more likely to result if the table is not crowded and children are not seated close to each other or in large groups. Babies and toddlers are more likely to stay at the table happily if they do not have to sit down until the food is ready and

Mealtimes are opportunities for exploring textures and consistencies as well as for eating.

cool enough to eat or wait until everyone is served or everyone is finished. They will also be helped to do this if the mealtime is organized for maximum independence and to encourage dexterity, for example, by making laying the table a key group activity. If small jugs with lids are used children can pour their own drinks without spilling.

Accidents will happen during the meal, so having everything to hand helps the practitioner deal with messes easily without having to keep jumping up from the table. Babies who have recently learnt to play at casting objects go through a lot of spoons! Non-verbal children may communicate that they have finished by pushing their plate away or even tipping food on the floor. If the key person eats with her key group s/he will anticipate potential difficulties and have regard for the idiosyncrasies of each child, thereby encouraging the kind of balance between playing and eating we observed with Sue, Paulette and Jack in Chapter 4.

Sleep and rest times

As children relax before dropping off to sleep they often chat and engage in verbal play, as Raj did in the observation in Chapter 3. Allowing ourselves to sleep in another's presence involves a high degree of trust. When we sleep we give up control and make ourselves vulnerable. At this vulnerable time babies and toddlers will be greatly helped to feel sufficiently relaxed if their key person follows their individual routines when settling them for sleep and is there when they wake. Naturally there will be times when a key worker is absent, but having another familiar adult present who knows their individual pattern will help the baby or toddler feel safe.

> Carla (10 months old) always played trampolining before she lay down to sleep. She bounces up and down holding on to the side of her cot while the other five babies are all soothed to sleep. Her key person said, 'Carla nearly always does a poo after lunch. She can't settle before this, so I always change and settle her down last. Perhaps the bouncing helps!'

Carla's key person had posted this information inside the cupboard door along with special information about all the babies in the group.

Sleep and rest times are also prime times for children's self-concept to be fostered. Keeping the routine predictable and maintaining the same layout of the rest mats or cots enables children to find their own places easily, to put away their own clothes and to find them again on waking. Toddlers quickly learn to identify who sleeps where and which is each child's bed cover and special object for sleep.

Home time

Conditions for play at home time are often neglected, with children grouped together in an unfamiliar space with unfamiliar adults in order to accommodate nursery shift patterns. Young children's resources for coping with being in a group situation may be low at this time of day and they may find it hard to play happily. Maintaining a familiar environment by ensuring the younger ones do not have to make too many changes will help. Young children feel more secure if they know what is happening.

> When Hannah is on the early shift she always makes a point of saying goodbye and telling her key children who will be looking after them. She also tells them if she is going to be away. They have a special box of clockwork toys and toys that make different noises that come out at the end of the day and each baby is washed and changed, ready to go home. She says that changing from being looked after by their key person to being in the care of their parent/carer can be quite an emotional time so they have put a lot of thought into supporting babies at this time, especially if parents/carers are late.

If children are expected to sit and wait with their coats on at the end of the day they may receive the message that they are a nuisance and are overstaying their welcome. Clearing up and stacking furniture in the proximity of the children may also have this negative effect. Adults may be familiar with being in this situation when eating in a restaurant just before closing time.

The impact of the environment on playing, growing and learning

> The carpeted floor had no tables and chairs. A large round solid foam shape, which was chest-high to many of the babies, provided a work surface that standing babies could steady themselves against as they played with the two or three telephones set out on it. Haru repeatedly climbed in and out of the small ball pool, casting balls out when inside and collecting

and dropping them in from the outside. Lucy and Katy were exploring the clear plastic tunnel. The adult support enabled them to do this without incident. They enjoyed crawling inside, backing out and patting the tunnel in excitement at the sight of each other.

A low slide/climbing frame was providing Jamie with a good view from a higher level, while David and Sian were sharing a den that had been created by replacing the doors of a low cupboard with curtains and the shelves inside with cushions. As usual Sian had chosen a selection of pieces from the inset puzzles on the low shelves and taken them in the den.

The skirting board around the room was being used as a display surface for photographs of individual babies and of activities and outings the group had done together. Another low poster on the wall showed photos of babies' families and pets, all of which were well thumbed. Jamie called and waved to his key person through the low window in the bathroom door as she changed another baby.

A rug in the corner of the room, beside a long low mirror, provided an interesting place for two immobile babies, Harry was batting the CDs hanging from the cord strung over the mat across that corner.

The observer of this environment noted that the baby room was a calm but dynamic play environment; babies from 3 months to 18 months were busy exploring. Adults were sitting on the floor around the room and on a low settee and were actively observing, chatting, playing and where necessary, offering a helping hand to the babies. Patrick Whitaker (2000) identifies two distinct types of environments in an organization – the invisible, psychological environment that is experienced mentally and emotionally by those within the organization and the physical environment that we experience with our senses.

The invisible, psychological play environment

If all the experiences children encounter have an impact on their play, growth and learning, then it is important that practitioners consider those that are invisible as well as the visible. Practitioners may be quite unconscious of this hidden curriculum, that is, the unplanned aspects of the provision, but nevertheless children will be learning a great deal from it. Many of the experiences of children from birth to three in daycare are unplanned and as we have emphasized previously they are drinking in all that surrounds them, particularly the actions and exchanges of their key adults and peers.

The amount of time and attention that adults give to different activities may suggest to children that some are more worthwhile. Enabling toddlers to help clear up after lunch may be viewed as less interesting and valuable than doing a 'messy play' activity. However, for the toddler helping in this way it may be every bit as exciting as the finger painting that the practitioner may have seen as the high point of the day. Compare the richness of the play experience of toddlers helping to put the rest mats out in the right places with the right personal blankets or transitional objects on each, with toddlers using shape sorters, and playing matching games. Children may also deduce from adults' behaviour that naming shapes and colours and counting are more important than pretend play or climbing, yet we have established the positive impact of imaginative and physical play on cognitive development and the acquisition of language.

Practitioners may play with some children more than others. Boys may attract more attention at the expense of girls or unacceptable behaviour may take up more of the practitioners' time than behaviour they approve of and would want to encourage. Children will be learning from all of these possibilities and those who get less attention may feel that they are less important to the adults. Play experiences and the environment may reflect only one cultural background, neglecting others; children may learn that things they are familiar with are not appreciated, or even acknowledged away from home (Drummond *et al.* 1989).

The curriculum is determined by and reflects the practitioners' preferences, values and beliefs and these are reflected in the physical environment they create. If practitioners hold the view that people need to conform to society through mastering a body of existing knowledge and regard children as empty vessels or blank sheets of paper and themselves as the providers of knowledge and the source of wisdom and authority in children's lives, then they will not view free-flowing, self-directed play as valuable. They would describe an appropriate play environment as one that is adult-controlled and where play experiences and learning are directed by the adult.

On the other hand, if practitioners believe that the world needs people who are self-directed, caring, creative, imaginative and able to adapt to change, and they regard children as whole people whose creativity and imagination must be encouraged, they will value play as a means of achieving this. Practitioners will create a play environment that is rich in resources, encourages exploration and discovery, helps children to use their initiative and act independently and allows children to make choices and solve problems (Drummond *et al.* 1989).

The physical play environment

The play environment is a critically important component of the curriculum and has a major impact on whether the needs of babies and toddlers can be met or not. Researchers suggest that space quality clearly predicts differences in practitioner behaviour and children's responses. High quality space is associated with sensitive and friendly practitioners and with interested and involved children. Low quality space is associated with neutral and insensitive practitioners and less involved and interested children and also with a high number of rules and restrictions (Howes *et al.* 1992).

Most of us have had experiences where our feelings and behaviour have altered in response to an environment, whether on entering a library, being in a department store in the January sales, at the fun fair, by the sea, or at home. Different environments are experienced as positive places to 'play' and feel comfortable for different people. If environments have such a powerful effect on adults, we can see how they have an even more powerful effect on very young

Environments that provide sensory experiences of soil, flowers, grass and trees are likely to be calming and enjoyable.

children whose senses are more alert and whose ability to cope with discomfort or stress is less. Young children's senses pick up on cues in the environment in ways adults have learned to process or ignore. They are unable to tune out at will. Moreover they cannot choose to leave and go elsewhere. Practitioners who try to ensure babies and toddlers have sensory experiences that are likely to be calming and enjoyable, with pleasant textures, smells and sounds such as water, soil, flowers, grass and trees, will provide rich environments for children.

When evaluating the environment in which young children will play, practitioners need to evaluate whether the environment is safe and familiar, or do the adults change it round every week? Does it reflect the children who use it – their homes, families and communities? Do the children know where things are and can they access them? All of these are important to address because they have a direct impact on:

- young children's emotional well-being and developing self-concept;
- young children's aesthetic sense and creativity;
- young children's need to feel empowered through impacting on their environment.

As well as the aesthetic and practical aspects of the environment practitioners also have to consider structural aspects such as group size, age range and adult/child ratios in the group. Howes *et al.* (1992) looked at both structural and process (interactions etc.) variables as indicators of 'thresholds of quality'. Their research showed that babies in groups of six or less and toddlers in groups of 12 or less were more likely to experience developmentally appropriate play opportunities. They also found that babies in a group with an adult/child ratio of 1:3 or less and toddlers in a group with a ratio of 1:4 or less were more likely to experience good care giving and good play experiences. Many practitioners working with children from birth to three report that these minimum ratios are frequently exceeded due to staff absences and shifts, often leaving them to care for more children than is recommended. They cite this as being the main impediment to them achieving the standards they are aiming for and the prime cause of their stress and frustration. The impact of such structural and organizational aspects of provision on the practitioner's ability to provide well for children's play cannot be ignored if high quality standards are to be achieved.

Features of the environment that foster close relationships

We have established babies' and toddlers' fundamental need for close relationships if they are to be confident in their play. Play environments created to foster this will have quiet, cosy corners both in and outdoors and protected space for non-mobile babies. The decor may be in calm colours and have cosy, textured fabrics, carpets and soft furnishings that provide a comfortable and comforting atmosphere. Rooms that are equipped with flexible lighting and room dividers will enable babies' individual sleep patterns to be followed while others play.

If the environment is designed so that it is not a thoroughfare for others in the building, children will be more able to concentrate on their play. This will also be aided if the number of times the key person has to leave the room can be reduced by the bathroom and feed preparation areas being en-suite and if viewing panels in the doors enable babies and key workers to remain in sight of each other. Low comfortable adult chairs support practitioners and also enable toddlers to climb up onto adult's laps. They make comfortable seating for parents too.

In the earlier observation of a nursery environment, the children's home experience was brought into the nursery environment by the displays at baby eye-level of photographs of the children, their families and other significant people. Fabrics, artefacts and resources from a range of cultures can be used, especially the play materials and equipment that practitioners know a child has at home such as an African-style sweeping brush or current TV toy. In one nursery parent/carers were invited to bring bedding from home so that the smell was familiar and cots were personalized with babies' own comforters and photographs of their family to contribute to their sense of well-being.

Features of the environment that support social skills and communication

Babies and toddlers enjoy playing with others, but because of their limited language, strong emotions and limited social skills conflicts can often arise. A well-planned play environment promotes and supports babies' and toddlers' growing self-awareness and ability to relate to and empathize with others. It can be organized to support children's play both alone and together by creating smaller enclosed areas and yet having plenty of space in other areas. This was seen in the baby room described in the observation, where one baby played in the ball pool while two babies shared the den in the cupboard. Babies, toddlers and older children also enjoy being able to see each other and meet together in communal areas. Furthermore, resources can be chosen that promote collaborative play, such as multisided easels, trucks with more than one seat and climbing frames with two parallel slides.

Features of the environment that empower moving and doing

We described babies and toddlers as playing and learning by moving and doing. Therefore they require much more free floor space for play than older children do. If the environment is sufficiently spacious and uncluttered it will support immature crawlers' and walkers' growing mobility. Using rugs as activity areas with clear space around them will enable children to move about safely and can create pathways to follow.

If the environment is interesting and stimulating from the eye level of the babies or toddlers it will inspire their play. An environment with different levels allows toddlers to experience being at different heights and to see different views, as Jamie in the observation was able to. Stage blocks can be used to make a raised play area.

The play environment in the observation did not contain tables and chairs. Babies interested in making sweeping arm movements and in casting toys will quickly clear a table of resources and then have nothing to do. Chairs will be seen as something to climb on or propel around the room. Toddlers may seem to change their minds about playing as soon as they have been seated on a chair and tucked under the table. Perhaps this makes them feel trapped and the need to move freely overrides their interest in the activity.

The predictability of the layout of furniture and resources facilitates play by providing stability and continuity for babies and toddlers. Adults will be familiar with the frustration of discovering products have been changed around in their local supermarket. A predictable environment enables children to form mental maps of their environment, to make choices and find favourite items and toddlers will be able to help the practitioner to tidy up. Individual pegs and storage for coats, nappies, shoes and comforters labelled with photographs and names will foster independence and a sense of belonging.

*Labelling individual children's items with
photographs and names fosters a sense of belonging.*

Environments that promote exploring, thinking and imagining

An environment for exploring, thinking and imagining includes resources that are both accessible and sufficiently open-ended for the children to use imaginatively. Workshop areas can be set up beside water and sand play trays, by using a row of vegetable racks or tubs on the floor placed in a row at right angles to a wall. These provide accessible storage and also define the area. Different types of materials like large pebbles, shells, twigs, and corks can be stored in the different sections and labelled with words and symbols. These materials can also be used in the home corner.

An appropriately stocked creativity and mark-making workshop can be created for toddlers. Chubby wax crayons, glue spreaders, film canisters of glue, hole punches, chubby pencils, round-ended scissors, paper bags, envelopes, different sized and textured paper will all offer this age group opportunities to become skilled tool users. It will enable them to find out about how materials such as paint, water and glue behave.

Thinking and imagining toddlers enjoy pretend play. However, some home corner furniture and resources may offer limited possibilities. More flexible resources such as a small bedside cupboard can be a cooker, fridge or a washing machine. A long low coffee table can be a dining table, a café table, a shop counter, or a baby-changing table. A low TV and video storage unit provides storage for a hairdressers' or doctor's equipment. How this furniture is used and the materials that are added should reflect the different cultures, changing interests and events in the lives of the children in the group.

The outdoor environment

The ideal outdoor environment is accessed directly from the group room so children can move freely between indoors and out. Very young children enjoy playing with nature, splashing in puddles, feeling and hearing the wind and rain or experiencing the contrast of sunshine and shade. One parent commented:

> A favourite game of Ryan's [23 months] is trying to sort out which bits of the shadows we cast are him and which are me.

Sensory pleasure and experience is gained from having interesting surfaces to touch, and to drag instruments along or bang, for example, with wooden spoons on picket fences. Children can enjoy these play experiences all year round if boots and warm waterproof clothes are available. Natural play space provides opportunities for the toddler to investigate natural materials like sand, mud, water, long grass and bushes. It has stones and logs to turn over and insects to find.

Overarching points

Few nurseries have ideal premises for the play of babies and toddlers. The authors have seen drab, uninspiring premises transformed however, by imaginative practitioners using fabrics and everyday resources and not necessarily by the purchase of expensive equipment. This creativity was also reflected in the quality and creativity of the babies' and toddlers' play. The most user-friendly environments for children from birth to three are tuned to individual babies' or toddlers' interests and the skills they are currently refining and developing. Practitioners working in a well-planned environment will feel more supported, valued and able to work to a high standard. Knowing what is excellent and having a wish list can help practitioners develop the play environment as and when they are able.

8

PARENTS AND PRACTITIONERS WORKING TOGETHER TO SUPPORT THE PLAY, GROWTH AND LEARNING OF CHILDREN FROM BIRTH TO THREE

We have to drive in to get here. In the morning if she's awake when she arrives, she's waving and blowing kisses at the building and she wants to be in here. You know, as a parent, that's a fantastic feeling. I would be filled with dread leaving her in a place where I either had some qualms or where she indicated in some way that she wasn't that happy about being here but that's never been the case. Her enthusiasm to be here is immense and I think it's testament to the system that's in place here . . . She's had the same key worker since she's been here . . . That's over a year.

(Parent of an 18-month-old attending a nursery centre,
Key Times Video 2001)

So far, the focus of this book has been on children from birth to three playing, growing and learning. The authors have established the importance of play and that children cannot fully immerse themselves in play if they are feeling insecure. As indicated in the parent's comments above, however, for children in daycare, the quality of the partnership between parents/carers and practitioners has a significant effect on that sense of security. Therefore in this chapter the focus is on the particular issues that arise for practitioners and parents/carers sharing the play, growth and learning of children from birth to three. These are:

• the social context of play provision for children from birth to three;
• parents/carers and practitioners helping the baby/toddler to settle and to play;

- parents/carers and practitioners sharing children's play;
- the support and development needs of practitioners.

If practitioners are truly to work in partnership with parents/carers, they need as clear an understanding as possible of what the issues might be for a parent/carer handing over their baby or toddler to someone else who will be playing with and caring for them. The decision parents/carers make about whether to use daycare for their baby is often influenced by factors such as their need to work or study. Becoming a parent/carer can awaken a strong desire to improve one's situation in order to better provide for one's child. Also becoming a parent/carer rarely excludes all other concerns and many adults feel more confident about being a good parent/carer if they maintain the stimulation of a career or academic studies. It can also stem from a parent/carer's belief that their child will have richer play and social experiences in a setting whose whole focus is on meeting the needs of young children.

The social context of play provision for children from birth to three

There are a number of overarching national, economic and political factors that will influence a parent/carer's decision about care for their young child. In contrast to some other European countries, social policy in Britain assumes that arrangements for the care and play provision of young children is the private concern of individual families (Moss in Pugh 1996). The idea of a more general public responsibility to our youngest citizens is not emphasized. It is only in cases where the family has totally broken down or has been assessed to be in need of additional support that financial resources from public funds are made available for daycare. Otherwise daycare provision for children from birth to three is via the private business sector, from which parents/carers purchase the care they need.

Such policies have been underpinned in the past by ideas that the proper place for young children's care and play is at home with their mothers and that daycare, especially in groups, is damaging for children's future development. For example, the Ministry of Health Circular 221/54 at the end of World War II stated:

under normal peace-time conditions the right policy to pursue would be positively to discourage mothers of children under two from going out to work, to make provision for children of between two and five by way of nursery schools and nursery classes; and to regard day nurseries and day guardians as supplements to meet special needs.

(Ministry of Health 1945)

We can see here the typical division between care and education, between younger and older children and between the full-time and part-time, public and private providers that are the different fragments of the jigsaw of present-day provision for young children in the UK.

The idea that it is better for young children's care and play to be home-based and provided by a parent persists. Yet this thinking has not resulted in social policies such as prolonged and adequately paid parental leave that would support parents/carers of young children spending time at home and having the time and opportunity to provide quality play experiences themselves. Meanwhile parents have needed to work or have required substitute care for their children for a range of reasons. This situation has meant that practitioners working with children from birth to three and parents using daycare for their young children have had to bear some uncertainty about whether or not they are providing the best for the children.

However, research carried out in Europe and the USA in the 1990s (see Moss and Melhuish 1991; Howes *et al.* 1992) emphasizes the importance of the *quality* of daycare for young children as the crucial issue that affects outcomes for children's development. This includes the quality of babies and toddlers' play experiences. Currently there is widespread support for developing and increasing provision, from policymakers as well as parents/carers. However, the new level of support from policymakers appears to be a response to the needs of the economy rather than recognition of the multifaceted social needs of children, parents and communities and the importance of good quality play provision in children's lives.

Government initiatives such as the National Childcare Strategy (DfEE 1998) and Working Families Tax Credit (Inland Revenue 2000) are designed to actively encourage parents into the workforce. Dahlberg *et al.* suggest that such policies reflect views of children as a 'labour market supply factor' (1999: 47), which must be addressed in order to release sufficient adults for work. Current policies result, they argue, in our early childhood settings being seen as either a means of social intervention that will produce a normalized child or as an extension of business, offered as an employee benefit that services the economy. They argue that early childhood settings can be more than a service provider and a business; they can be forums 'in which children and adults participate together in projects of social, cultural, political and economic significance' (1999: 73), which would imply having children's play as a central focus. To be a forum in a civil society, however, requires that settings be open to all families with young children whatever their circumstances. Therefore the setting must be publicly resourced, much in the way that provision for children over 3 in 'education' settings is at least partially publicly resourced through the Nursery Education Grant.

In a framework of publicly resourced, equally accessible provision the emphasis on 'What provision?', 'How much provision?' and 'Who is it for?' is reduced, allowing a discourse to emerge that is centred on the detail of how children, parents and practitioners can construct 'a place for children to live their childhoods' (Dahlberg *et al.* 1999: 75) by answering such questions as, 'What rich opportunities can be provided for young children to play, grow and learn?'

Parents/carers and practitioners helping the baby/toddler to settle and to play

Regardless of how rich a play environment the daycare setting is, separation and loss for a new child will be inherent to the process of entering daycare either in a group or with a childminder. A well-planned settling-in period minimizes the distress of the child by helping them to start to make new attachments to the key person while gradually separating from their parents/carers over a period of time. Then and only then will the child be able to benefit from the opportunities available for play and learning. This process needs careful and sensitive handling; indeed, one group of staff described it as the most important piece of work that they do. They also described the purpose of settling in as 'to build bridges between the key person and the child and parent/carer and between home and nursery' (Manning-Morton and Thorp 2001, sect. 1: 9). Parents/carers will need to be forewarned of this gradual process so they can be available for sufficient time and know what to expect. What happens in the settling-in period can set the tone for the future relationship between all concerned.

Home visits

These can build familiarity for the child in a safe context. Taking a few carefully chosen toys can provide an enjoyable play experience and act as a point of focus for the child that is less daunting than a strange new person. One nursery, using a play bag at the home visit on a Friday, would leave one of the treasures from the bag at the child's home for the child to bring in on their first day, the following Monday. If a parent declines a home visit, the same amount of time and attention can be given to their introductory visit to the setting. This is a good time to discover how a child plays, and what their current interests and schemas might be, as described by Liam's mother in the comment recorded below.

Playing with the new baby or toddler

As well as finding out about the child at a home or introductory visit, playing with the baby or toddler gives the key person a picture of the whole child and an understanding of their culture. In addition to home languages, family composition and ethnicity, a young child's culture includes the way physical care is given, the interactive games the parent/carer and child play, favourite playthings, books, songs, TV programmes or videos.

A welcoming atmosphere

The key person greeting both the parent/carer and child on their first day and every day by their proper or chosen names will create a welcoming atmosphere. Having items such as coat pegs and personal bags already labelled creates an impression of care and belonging. Key workers can use the cultural knowledge they have acquired from the home visit to prepare play experiences that are tuned to that child. The authors recorded the following comment from a parent.

> When we had our home visit I explained about Liam's play, how he loves pottering round the flat trailing anything with a flex behind him, like the vacuum cleaner or my hair drier. On his first day Leon [the key worker] had put out lengths of string tied to little toys, and in the garden there were lengths of garden hose. I was amazed and touched at the care and interest he'd taken.
>
> (Manning-Morton and Thorp 2001)

Becoming a trusted adult

Becoming a trusted adult and secure base for the child is the primary aim of the key person. In order for this to happen the parent must be there but sit back and allow room for that relationship to develop alongside their own. The baby's or toddler's trust of the key person can be gradually built through play. The child will need space and the key person must respect hard stares and other messages communicating their wariness. The toddler will be more comfortable if they can initiate any physical contact in these early days. The young baby will feel more secure if the parent's way of holding is imitated. Tiny babies' sense of smell is well developed and a key worker who drapes something of the parent's across her or him when bottle-feeding may find the baby settles more easily (Manning-Morton and Thorp 2001).

Separating

This will be made as smooth and painless as possible if the key person and child have been playing together well before the parent/carer says goodbye. After following whatever goodbye ritual the child finds helpful, that same play can be returned to and the memory of it having recently been a positive experience may help calm and engage the child. Holding or staying near the child if they are distressed, acknowledging the distressed feelings and putting

After following the child's own goodbye ritual, the key person and child can return to play.

these into words for them will be of more comfort than immediate attempts at distraction. Using a familiar milestone such as 'after we have had a play and some lunch', to tell the child when the parent is returning will be more meaningful than saying they will be back later.

Careful observation

Observation and record-keeping will enable the key person to feed-back specific information to the parent/carer each day about their child's play and general well-being. Daily adjustments can be made to keep the settling-in process going well if the communication channels are kept open. Both practitioner and parent/carer can feel guilty or be tempted to blame the other if the child is finding this time difficult. Tension between the adults closest to the child will exacerbate any insecurity they may be feeling. Parents and practitioners who incorporate their learning about each other's games and play experiences into their own interaction with the baby or toddler will be strengthening the child's sense of security.

Supporting the parent/carer

It is equally important that careful planning goes into what is happening for the parents/carers at this time. Parents/carers may have some very ambivalent feelings in these early days of separating from their baby or toddler. One possible tension parents/carers might experience at this time may be a strong desire for their child to feel safe and enjoy playing with the key person, while simultaneously feeling anxious that the child might grow to prefer the practitioner. Elinor Goldschmied recommends that the practitioner explain that sharing love is not like sharing an apple; the love a child gives to one person does not lessen the amount available to anyone else (Goldschmied and Jackson 1994).

If time is taken to discuss the settling-in period well before the process begins, then difficulties arising from different expectations of what this means in practice will be alleviated. It helps a parent/carer appreciate and support the building of a close relationship between the practitioner and their child if they understand that this is essential for their child's security and will enable their baby or toddler to play and learn. Negotiating the best way of parting beforehand is important. Much bad feeling will be avoided if it is explained that multiple goodbyes, or parents/carers sneaking out or frequently peeping back so the child keeps seeing glimpses of them can exacerbate the child's distress.

When parents/carers return, rather than compounding their fears of losing their child's love by saying things like: 'He's been really happy all day. He didn't miss you at all!' Goldschmied and Jackson (1994) point out a key person's more sensitive, and probably accurate approach, might be:

> There were times when Liam did get upset and look a bit lost, but by giving him your photo and his blanket from home I was able to comfort him and soon he was playing happily again.

Getting the balance right

Goldschmied and Jackson point out that it is important to be realistic and not to promise what cannot be delivered. Sometimes the key person, in their desire to be supportive to the parent/carer may make extravagant offers. They give the example of saying: 'come and talk to me at any time' (Goldschmied and Jackson 1994). Instead, having regular set times for discussion about their children's play, growth and learning will be appreciated by busy parents, and practitioners will be clear about who they are focusing on at particular times and not feel overwhelmed.

These basic, practical steps can make the early days of separating much less stressful. They enable a parent/carer to get to know their child's key person and see them at work and to have their views included. They help parent/carers appreciate and value the play experiences their child is being offered and to understand that play only happens in the right circumstances.

Colleagues' support for each other

Colleagues' support for each other is extremely valuable, especially when one practitioner is settling or comforting a child and building a relationship of trust with the parent/carer. Staff who trust and respect each other can share thoughts, feelings and ideas about how each may best support the child's needs and those of the parent/carer. The key person also needs extra support from their line manager at this time. Time for the key worker to discuss their feelings is helpful as they may be the one who is not only containing the child's feelings but the parents/carer's feelings as well.

Staff who trust and respect each other can share thoughts, feelings and ideas about how best to support children's and parent/carer's needs.

Parents/carers sharing in children's play, growth and learning

There is no such species as 'the parent' or 'the carer'. It is unhelpful for practitioners to generalize about parents/carers. The cultural diversity (in the widest sense of the word) of those using daycare must be recognized. It follows therefore, that parents/carers will have a variety of different expectations, especially with regard to the value and type of play experiences and degree of independence they see as

Table 8.1 Families have different beliefs about:

What is or is not important
What behaviour is or is not acceptable
Worldviews
How ideas are expressed and passed on
Clothes
Diet
Religion and spirituality
Relationships

Table 8.2 In relation to babies and toddlers, the following are common areas where expectations vary and there is potential for conflict between practitioners and parents/carers:

Attitudes to education and the importance of play
Setting limits
Physical handling
Gender roles
Appropriate clothing
Food and feeding
Sleeping routines
Outdoor play
Messy play
Children's independence
Potty training

---

appropriate for children from birth to three. Therefore the importance of practitioners' 'careful examination of their own attitudes towards the families they work with' (A'Beckett in Stonehouse 1988: 142) cannot be emphasized too strongly. Practitioners will understand the value of using such resources as the Treasure Basket, Heuristic Play, play with paint or cornflour and outdoor play. However, these may be alien concepts to parents/carers new to the setting and need explanation. A practitioner cannot presume that parents/carers will have prior knowledge and understanding of what good quality early play experiences are, neither should they assume that parents/carers have no idea. Parents/carers who appreciate the play experiences being offered may use ideas from the setting at home and bring things from home to contribute to the group's resources. This will directly benefit the baby or toddler.

Ways of sharing ideas about children's play

Cath Arnold (in Whalley 1997) describes different ways of sharing ideas about how children play and learn with parents/carers and ways to encourage parents/carers to share information about their own children's play and learning. Athey observed that there is nothing more likely to interest parents/carers than the "illumination of his or her child's own behaviour" (1990: 66). Some of Arnold's ideas include:

- Take some photos of children you know well and ask their parents/carers what they think they are doing.
- Consult the parents/carers of a child you are struggling to provide

for, and ask for their suggestions. Be honest with them. They will appreciate you recognizing their greater knowledge of their own child.

- Prepare a display and consult parents/carers about which photos to include.
- Set up a small project and focus on one key issue. Ask parents/carers to meet you each week to gather evidence of, for example, high involvement or a particular schema.

(Arnold in Whalley 1997: 57)

Parents/carers playing and learning

Some settings for children from birth to three organize parent/carers' evenings with the baby and toddler rooms prepared for play and key workers sited in different areas. They have information displayed about each area, describing why it is organized in that way and what the children gain from playing there. They display photographs of children using the area alongside the explanations. As parents/carers arrive they are invited to try using the materials available. Although some may feel self-conscious at first, barriers soon come down and some parents/carers have fun as well as learning a lot about what their children do and why. These evenings also raise parents/carers' appreciation of practitioners' depth of knowledge, skill and planning. Great enjoyment, much conversation and even stronger nursery–home links will be forged if parents' models, paintings and any photographs taken of them making these, are labelled and displayed for when the children come in the next day.

Play at home

Inviting parents/carers to read stories, to use a special skill they have or to come on outings are widely established ways of including parents/carers in their child's play and learning. However, it is important to recognize the importance of the play that takes place at home. Some parents/carers may enjoy making audio tape recordings, videos and taking photographs to record particular events, schemas, interests or abilities children have and to share these with practitioners.

So rather than key worker and parents/carers taking alternating shifts and having little influence on each other, we can see that a lot can be done to make shared care an integrated process that provides continuity of experience for the children.

The importance of practitioners who work with children from birth to three

Throughout this book we have emphasized the importance of the first three years of life and the impact the quality of the environment can have on the play, growth and learning of children from birth to three. But we also underline that practitioners play a crucially important role in children's lives. The work of practitioners caring for children from birth to three can have more impact on the emerging personality of their charges than any university lecturer has on their students. For this reason we have included a section on the role of the adult in babies' and toddlers' play in each of the preceding chapters, as we believe that the practitioner is the prime factor in affecting the variability of quality contexts.

The characteristics of babies and toddlers and the quality of care they should be able to expect, require practitioners who have particular and special skills and characteristics of their own. They need to be tuned in, sensitive, respectful and knowledgeable about children from birth to three (Stonehouse 1988). Through our work with many practitioners caring for children from birth to three, we have come to believe that they also need to be enthusiastic and motivated about their work, reflective of their practice, have emotional conviction as well as intellectual knowledge about good practice and be aware of their personal motivations, values, beliefs and experiences that affect their practice. They need to have a broad knowledge of play and developmental theory and the kind of interpersonal and intrapersonal skills that enable them to play effectively with babies and toddlers and to build positive relationships with parents/carers.

These are important areas of skill and knowledge, necessary to providing proper emotional care and appropriate play experiences in a professional context. Practitioners working with children from birth to three undertake an arduous, demanding and complex task that requires high levels of skill, a depth of knowledge and a wide range of abilities. It is a highly responsible job that requires a mature approach to understanding oneself and others and the ability to reflect on actions and feelings. Goleman (1996) would describe this as having emotional intelligence.

Professional worth

Despite its obvious importance the ambivalence on the part of the UK government towards investing in daycare for children from birth to three has created uncertainty for practitioners as to the validity of their role, which can make it hard for them to be confident in their practice and to develop a sense of professionalism and pride. In addition the pay, conditions and training of many workers with young children are poor, the worst of them occurring among those working with children from birth to three, particularly in privately provided services (Moss in Pugh 1996). A report on private day nurseries in the UK concludes that the quality of care for children aged 2 and under is directly linked to pay and conditions of work of staff, and to staff support and training (Penn 1994).

This lack of external validation can lead to a negative sense of professional worth, which impacts negatively on practice. There is a clear link between the well-being of the child and the well-being of the practitioner, often manifested in the quality of the play opportunities and interactions that take place in a setting. Practitioners who are respected, valued and supported in developing their practice are committed to providing well for children's play. Therefore, recognition of their important role through ongoing professional support, adequate pay and conditions and improved training and qualification opportunities is fundamental to developing quality provision.

The care of young children in group or childminding settings is a profession. In our view this kind of professionalism does not equate with instrumentality (thinking, rationality and logic) and ignore the nurturing and affective (feeling and emotion) aspects of this work. An overemphasis on the cognitive and on education and learning can result in the nurturing role not being encouraged as professional, which can result in a lack of adequate concern for the emotional well-being of young children and a formal, instructive approach to children's play. Practitioners who are able to articulate why the detail of *all* of the children's care and play experiences are central to children's learning, maintain their credibility as educators in the broadest sense.

Support, development and change

For the successful implementation of a truly broad and balanced curriculum, practitioners need to be given sufficient time and space to:

- discuss each individual child's development and interests;
- consider the detail of play opportunities, routines and environment;
- share information with parents/carers.

This takes place in a cycle of good practice consisting of observing, planning and evaluating children's play experiences. Practitioners also need time and space to: 'Reflect on the emotional ideas inherent in practice and its relationship to their own personal experience' (Manning-Morton 2000b).

This process should be a dialogue within which a cycle of reflective practice takes place. The support practitioners need in providing responsive care and forming key person relationships with children requires sufficient external supports that 'contain' the practitioner. This is effective if it takes place in a cycle of emotionally intelligent practice as shown in Figure 8.1. In this cycle you cannot address the needs of the children without addressing the physical, emotional and learning needs of the adults. The characteristics of children from birth to three require the development of key person relationships. This demands high levels of interpersonal and intrapersonal skills on the part of the practitioner, which in turn require effective support systems from the organization. In this way practitioners are enabled to respond to the children's characteristics effectively.

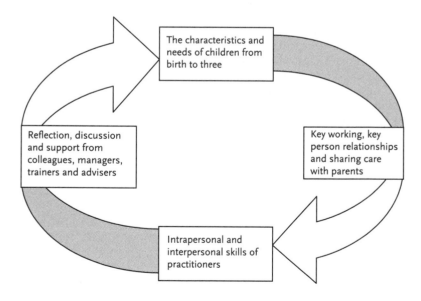

Figure 8.1 A cycle of emotionally intelligent practice

These are the kind of support systems practitioners are looking for:

'Regular appraisal, support and supervision sessions from my manager.'
'Reassurance, am I getting it right?'
'To be heard by the 'Top'.
'Time to reflect with my colleagues and evaluate the work.'
'Time and space to share knowledge and skills with colleagues and parents/carers.'
'Training and personal development.'
(Members of the London Borough of Camden Under Threes
Development Group (Manning-Morton 2000b))

Training programmes that encourage reflective practice, as well as broadening practitioners' knowledge and skills, support practitioners in feeling confident about their practice. This in turn can only improve external views of the role and status of the practitioner working with children from birth to three.

Developing high quality play provision for children from birth to three means paying attention to both the dynamic aspects of provision, such as the daily interactions in play and also to the structural aspects, such as adult–child ratios and training (Williams 1995). Practitioners and providers can all influence the dynamic aspects of quality, as individuals and as groups. In developing professional skills and knowledge practitioners may also influence the organizational aspects of quality at a local level. Influencing structural change on a wider level, however, requires a more long-term campaign of lobbying to persuade those without the professional knowledge to value children's play and prioritize the well-being of young children as the responsibility of our whole society.

REFERENCES

Abbott, L. and Moylett, H. (1997) *Working with the Under-3's: Responding to Children's Needs*. Buckingham: Open University Press.

Acredolo, L. and Goodwyn, S. (1985) Symbolic gesturing in language development: A case study. *Human Development*, 28: 40–9.

Acredolo, L. and Goodwyn, S. (2000) *Baby Signs. How to Talk with Your Baby Before Your Baby Can Talk*. London: Vermilion, Ebury Press.

Ainsworth, M., Blehar, M., Waters, E. and Wall, S. (1978) *Patterns of Attachment: Assessed in the Strange Situation and at Home*. Hillside, NJ: Erlbaum.

Athey, C. (1990) *Extending Thought in Young Children*. London: Paul Chapman.

Axline, V. (1964) *Dibs: In Search of Self*. Middlesex: Penguin.

Bain, A. and Barnett, L. (1980) *The Design of a Day Care System in a Nursery Setting for Children Under Five*. London: Tavistock Institute for Human Relations.

Barbara Hepworth Museum (1977) *Some Statements by Barbara Hepworth*. St Ives, Cornwall: Trewyn Studio and Garden.

Barnard, C. and Meldis, S. (2000) *Playsense for Play for Babies and Toddlers: A Resource Pack*. London: Play Matters National Association of Toy and Leisure Libraries.

Bates, E., O'Connell, B. and Shore, C. (1987) Languages and communication in infancy, in J.D. Osalsky (ed.) *Handbook of Infant Development*, 2nd edn. New York: Wiley.

Bee, H. (2000) *The Developing Child*, 9th edn. Boston, MA: Allyn and Bacon.

Belsky, J. (1988) The effects of infant daycare reconsidered. *Early Childhood Research Quarterly*, 3: 235–82.

Blakemore, C. (1998) *The Mind Machine.* London: BBC Books.

Bohannon, J.N. III, and Warren-Leubecker, A. (1988) Recent developments in child directed speech, we've come a long way, baby-talk. *Language Sciences,* 10: 89–110.

Bowlby, J. (1965) *Child Care and the Growth of Love.* London: Penguin.

Bowlby, J. (1969) *Attachment and Loss, Vol. 1: Attachment.* London: Hogarth.

Bowlby, J. (1973) *Attachment and Loss, Vol. 2: Separation.* Harmondsworth, Middlesex: Penguin.

Bowlby, J. (1979) *The Making and Breaking of Affectional Bonds.* London: Tavistock/Routledge.

Bowlby, J. (1988) *A Secure Base: Clinical Applications of Attachment Theory.* London: Routledge.

Brown, B. (2001) *Combatting Discrimination: Persona Dolls in Action.* London: Trentham Books.

Bruce, T. (1991) *Time to Play in Early Childhood Education.* London: Hodder and Stoughton.

Bruce, T. (1997) *Early Childhood Education.* London: Hodder and Stoughton.

Bruce, T. and Meggitt, C. (1996) *Childcare and Education.* London: Hodder and Stoughton.

Bruner, J.S. (1966) *Toward a Theory of Instruction.* Cambridge, MA: Harvard University Press.

Bruner, J.S. (1977) Early social interaction and language ascquisition, in H.R. Schaffer (ed.) *Studies of Mother–Infant Interaction.* London: Academic Press.

Bruner, J. and Sherwood, V. (1975) Peekaboo and the learning of rule structures, in J. Bruner, A. Jolly, and K. Sylva (eds) (1976) *Play and Its Role in Development and Evolution.* Harmondworth, Middlesex: Penguin.

Carle, F. (1984) *Brown Bear, Brown Bear, What Do You See?* London: Penguin.

Carter, R. (1999) *Mapping the Mind.* London: Seven Dials.

Creasey, G.L., Jarvis, P.A. and Berk, L.E. (1998) Play and social competence, in O.N. Saracho and B. Spodek (eds) (1998) *Multiple Perspectives on Play in Early Childhood Education.* Albany, NY: SUNY Press.

Dahlberg, G., Moss, P. and Pence, A. (1999) *Beyond Quality in Early Childhood Education and Care.* London: Falmer Press.

Davies, M. (1995/2000) *Helping Children to Learn through a Movement Perspective.* London: Hodder and Stoughton.

Department for Education and Employment (DfEE) (1998) *Meeting the Childcare Challenge, A Framework and Consultation Document.* London: HMSO.

Derman-Sparks, L. (1989) *Anti-Bias Curriculum*. Washington DC: National Association for the Education of Young Children.

Drummond, M-J., Lally, M. and Pugh, G. (eds) (1989) *Working with Children. Developing a Curriculum in the Early Years.* London: National Children's Bureau/Nottingham group.

Duffy, B. (1998) *Supporting Creativity and Imagination in the Early Years.* Buckingham: Open University Press.

Dunn, J. (1988) *The Beginnings of Social Understanding.* Oxford: Blackwell.

Dunn, J. and Kendrick, C. (1982) *Siblings: Love, Envy and Understanding.* Cambridge, MA: Harvard University Press.

Elfer, P. (1996) Building intimacy in relationships with young children in nurseries. *Early Years,* 16 (2): 30–4.

Elfer, P., Goldschmied, E. and Selleck, D. (2002) *Key Person Relationships in Nursery.* London: National Early Years Network.

Eliot, L. (1999) *Early Intelligence. How the Brain and Mind Develop in the First Five Years of Life.* London: Penguin.

Fernald, A., Taeschner, T., Dunn, J., Papousek, M., Boyssen-Bardies, B. and Fukui, I. (1989) A cross language study of prosodic modification in mother's and father's speech to pre-verbal infants. *Journal of Child Language,* 16: 477–502.

Free Kindergarten Association (FKA) (1991) *Bi-lingual Staff Work!* Multi-cultural Resource Centre Australia (video).

Gambetti, A. (2000) Lecture, Reggio Emilia Preschools and Infant–Toddler Centres. UK Study Week, October.

Garvey, C. (1990) *Play,* 2nd edn. Cambridge, MA: Harvard University Press.

Gibson, E.J. and Walk, R.D. (1960) The visual cliff. *Scientific American,* 202: 64–71.

Goddard, S. (2002) *Reflexes, Learning and Behaviour.* Eugene, OR: Fern Ridge Press.

Goldschmied, E. and Jackson, S. (1994) *People Under Three, Young Children in Day Care.* London: Routledge.

Goldschmied, E. and Selleck, D. (1996) *Communication between Babies in Their First Year* (video). London: National Children's Bureau.

Goleman, D. (1996) *Emotional Intelligence: Why It Can Matter More Than IQ.* London: Bloomsbury Publishing.

Göncü, A. (1993) Development of intersubjectivity in social pretend play, in M. Woodhead, D. Faulkner and K. Littleton (eds) (1998) *Cultural Worlds of Early Childhood.* London: Routledge.

Goossens, F. and Van Ijzendoorn, M. (1990) Quality of infants' attachments to professional caregivers. *Child Development,* 61: 832–7.

Gopnik, A., Meltzoff, A. and Kuhl, P. (1999) *How Babies Think*. London: Weidenfield and Nicolson.

Goswami, U. (1998) *Cognition in Children*. Hove, Sussex: Psychology Press.

Greenman, J. and Stonehouse, A. (1996) *Prime Times. A Handbook for Excellence in Infant Toddler Programs*. St. Paul, MN: Redleaf Press.

Gussin-Paley, V. (2001) *In Mrs. Tulley's Room. A Childcare Portrait*. Cambridge, MA: Harvard University Press.

Halliday, M. (1975) *Learning How to Mean*. London: Arnold.

Holmes, J. (1993) *John Bowlby and Attachment Theory*. London: Routledge.

Hopkins, J. (1988) Facilitating the development of intimacy between nurses and infants in day nurseries. *Early Child Development and Care*, 33: 99–111.

Howes, C., Phillips, D.A. and Whitebook, M. (1992) Thresholds of quality: implications for the social development of children in centre-based childcare. *Child Development*, 63: 449–60.

Hutt, J.F., Tyler, S., Hutt, C. and Christopherson, H. (1989) *Play, Exploration and Learning: A Natural History of Pre-School*. London: Routledge.

Inland Revenue (2000) *Working Families Tax Credit, Marketing and Communications*. London: HMSO.

Isaacs, S. (1929) *The Nursery Years*. London: Routledge.

Karmiloff-Smith, A. (1994) *Baby It's You*. London: Ebury Press.

Karmiloff-Smith, A. (1995) The extraordinary journey from foetus through infancy. *Journal of Child Psychology and Psychiatry*, 36: 1293–315.

Katz, L. (1988) What should young children be doing? *American Educator*. Summer: 28–33, 44–5.

Klein, M. (1932) *The Psychoanalysis of Children*. London: Hogarth.

Kraemer, S. (2000) Promoting Resilience in Children: The mistakes we must not make at a turning point in history. *International Journal of Child and Family Welfare*. Vol. 4, part 3, pp. 273–8.

Laakso, M-L. (1999) Early intentional communication as a predictor of language development in young toddlers. *First Language*, 19 (2): 2070–231.

Laevers, F. (ed.) (1994) *The Leuven Involvement Scale for Young Children*. Leuven, Belgium: Centre for Experiential Education.

Laevers, F., Vandenbussche, E., Kog, M. and Depondt, L. (1997) *A Process Oriented Child Monitoring System for Young Children*. Leuven, Belgium: Centre for Experiential Education.

Lally, J.R., Torres, Y.L. and Phelps, P.C. (1997) Caring for infants and toddlers in groups: Necessary considerations for emotional, social and cognitive development. *Zero to Three*, 14(5): 1–8. www.zerotothree.org.

Lieberman, A. (1993) *The Emotional Life of the Toddler*. New York: Free Press.

McMahon, L. (1994) Therapeutic play for young children. Helping children manage their feelings and behaviour. *Early Years*, 14 (2): 30–3.

Mandler, J.M. (1992) How to build a baby II: Conceptual primitives. *Psychological Review*, 99: 587–604.

Mandler, J.M. (1996) Pre-verbal Representation and Language, in P. Bloom, M. Peterson, L. Nadel and M. Garrett (eds) *Language and Space*. London: Bradford Books.

Manning-Morton, J. (2000a) Transition: A Parent and Child Settling into Day Care. Case Study Presentation at Pen Green Conference, Pen Green Training, Development and Research Base, Corby, Northants, March.

Manning-Morton, J. (2000b) 'Working with children under three. Intimacy, trust and well-being in the nursery.' Unpublished MA dissertation. University of North London.

Manning-Morton, J. and Thorp, M. (2000) *Working with Children from Birth to Three, A Distance Learner's Handbook*. London University of North London.

Manning-Morton, J. and Thorp, M. (2001) *Key Times: A Framework for Developing High Quality Provision for Children under Three Years*. London: Camden EYDCP/University of North London.

Marshall, T. (1982) Infant care: A day nursery under the microscope. *Social Work Service*, 32: 15–32.

Matthews, J. (1994) *Helping Children to Draw and Paint in Early Childhood*. London: Hodder and Stoughton.

Matthews, J. (1999) How adult companions give children a 'Sure Start' for their early learning. *Early Childhood Practice*. 1 (1): 73–80.

Maude, P. (2001) *Physical Children, Active Teaching: Investigating Physical Literacy*. Buckingham: Open University Press.

Meade, A. (1995) Presentation to the Early Childhood Convention. New Zealand, September 1995.

Meek, M. (1985) Play and paradoxes: Some considerations for imagination and language, in G. Wells and J. Nicholls (eds) *Language and Learning: An International Perspective*. London: Falmer Press.

Meltzoff, A.N. and Moore, M.K. (1983) Newborn infants' imitation of adult facial gestures. *Child Development*, 54: 702–9.

Mental Health Foundation (1999) *Bright Futures. Promoting Children and Young People's Mental Health*. London: The Mental Health Foundation.

Miller, L., Rustin, M. and Shuttleworth, J. (eds) (1989) *Closely Observed Infants*. London: Duckworth.

Ministry of Health (1945) *Circular 221/54*. London: HMSO.

Moss, P. and Melhuish, E. (eds) (1991) *Current Issues in Day Care for Young Children*. London: HMSO.

Moyles, J. (1989) *Just Playing? The Role and Status of Play in Early Childhood Education*. Buckingham: Open University Press.

Parten, M. (1932) Social participation among pre-school children. *Journal of Abnormal and Social Psychology*, 27: 243–69.

Penn, H. (1994) *Private Nurseries in the UK*, a Report for BBC News and Current Affairs, Panorama. Institute of Education, University of London. National Children's Bureau.

Perris, E.E., Myers, N.A. and Clifton, R.K. (1990) Long term memory for a single infancy experience. *Child Development*, 61: 1796–807.

Piaget, J. (1926) *The Language of Thought and the Child*. New York: Harcourt, Brace and World.

Piaget, J. (1952) *The Origin of Intelligence in the Child*. London: Routledge and Kegan Paul.

Piaget, J. (1962) *Play, Dreams and Imitation in Childhood*. London: Routledge and Kegan Paul.

Piaget, J. and Inhelder, B. (1969) *The Psychology of the Child*. London: Routledge and Kegan Paul.

Pugh, G. (ed.) (1996) *Contemporary Issues In The Early Years: Working Collaboratively For Children*. London: National Children's Bureau/ Paul Chapman.

Purkey, W. (1970) *Self-concept and School Achievement*. London: Paul Chapman.

Qualifications and Curriculum Authority/Department of Education and Employment (QCA/DfEE) (2000) *Curriculum Guidance for the Foundation Stage*. London: HMSO.

Rader, N., Bausano, M. and Richards, J.E. (1980) On the nature of the visual cliff avoidance response in human infants. *Child Development*, 51: 61–6.

Raikes, H. (1993) Relationship duration in infant care: Time with a high-ability teacher and infant–teacher attachment. *Early Childhood Research Quarterly*, 8: 309–25.

Robertson, J. and Robertson, J. (1953) *A Two Year Old Goes to Hospital* (film). London: Tavistock Child Development Research Unit.

Rosen, M. and Oxenbury, H. (1989) *We're Going on a Bear Hunt*. London: Walker Books.

Rowlett, W. (2000) 'To what degree does mobility enrich the personal, social and emotional development, within the outside play curriculum for children under three?' BA (Hons) Degree Project. University of North London.

Rubin, J.Z., Provenzano, F.J. and Luria, Z. (1974) The eye of the beholder: Parents' views on the sex of newborns. *American Journal of Orthopsychiatry*, 44: 512–19.

Rutter, M. (1995) Clinical implications of attachment concepts: Retrospect and prospect. *Journal of Child Psychology and Psychiatry*, 36 (4): 549–71.

Saracho, O.N. and Spodek, B. (eds) (1998) *Multiple Perspectives on Play in Early Childhood Education*. Albany, NY: SUNY Press.

Schaffer, H.R. and Emerson, P.E. (1964) The developments of social attachments in infancy. *Monographs of the Society for Research in Child Development*, 29.

Schore, A.N. (2001) Effects of a secure attachment relationship on right brain development, affect regulation and infant mental health. *Infant Mental Health Journal*. Vol. 22, Issue 1–2, 7–66.

Selleck, D. (1997) Baby art: Art is me, in P. Gura (ed.) *Reflections on Early Education and Care*. London: British Association for Early Childhood Education.

Sharp, P. (2001) *Nurturing Emotional Literacy*. London: Fulton.

Shuttleworth, J. (1989) Psychoanalytic theory and infant development, in L. Miller, M. Rustin and J. Shuttleworth (eds) *Closely Observed Infants*. London: Duckworth.

Siegal, D.J. (1999) *The Developing Mind*. New York: Guilford Press.

Siraj-Blatchford, I. (1994) *The Early Years: Laying the Foundations for Racial Equality*. London: Trentham Books.

Siraj-Blatchford, I. and Clarke, P. (2000) *Supporting Identity, Diversity and Language in the Early Years*. Buckingham: Open University Press.

Slade, A. (1987) A longitudinal study of maternal involvement and symbolic play during the toddler period. *Child Development*, 58: 367–75.

Smith, B.A. and Lloyd, J. (1978) Maternal behaviour and perceived sex of infant revisited. *Child Development*, 46: 1263–5.

Smith, P.K., Cowie, H. and Blades, M. (1998) *Understanding Children's Development*, 3rd edn. Oxford: Blackwell

Smolucha, F. (1991) Mother's verbal scaffolding of pretend play, in R.M. Diaz and L.E. Berk (eds) *Private Speech: From Social Interaction to Self-Regulation*. Hillside, NJ: Erlbaum.

Stern, D. (1990) *Diary of a Baby*. London: Fontana.

Stonehouse, A. (ed.) (1988) *Trusting Toddlers; Programming for 1–3 year olds in Childcare Centres*. Melbourne: Australian Early Childhood Association.

Sure Start (2002) *Birth to Three Matters: A framework to support children in their earliest years*. London: DfES.

Talay-Ongen, A. (1998) *Typical and Atypical Development in Early Childhood. The Fundamentals*. England: BPS Books.

Thomas, A. and Chess, S. (1980) *The Dynamics of Psychological Development*. New York: Bruner/Mozel.

Trevarthan, C. (1979) Communication and co-operation in early infancy: A description of intersubjectivity, in: M. Bullowa (ed.) *Before Speech: The Beginning of Interpersonal Communication*. Cambridge: Cambridge University Press.

Trevarthan, C. (1993) The function of emotions in early infant communication and development, in J. Nadel and L. Carmaioni (eds) *New Perspectives in Early Communicative Development*. London: Routledge.

Trevarthan, C. (1995) The child's need to learn a culture, in M. Woodhead, D. Faulkner and K. Littleton (eds) (1998) *Cultural Worlds of Early Childhood*. London: Routledge.

Trevarthan, C. and Malloch, S. (2002) Musicality and music before three. *Zero to Three*, September.

Vygotsky, L.S. (1966) Play and its role in the mental development of the child, in J. Bruner, A. Jolly and K. Sylva (eds) (1976) *Play and its Role in Development and Evolution*. Harmondsworth, Middlesex: Penguin.

Vygotsky, L.S. (1978) *Mind in Society*. Cambridge, MA: Harvard University Press.

Vygotsky, L.S. (1986) *Thought and Language*. Cambridge, MA: MIT Press.

Weir, R. (1962) *Language in the Crib*. The Hague: Mouton.

Whalley. M. (ed.) (1997) *Working with Parents*. London: Hodder and Stoughton.

Whitaker, P. (2000) *Management in the Early Years: Challenges and Responsibilities. A Distance Learner's Handbook*. London: University of North London.

Whitehead, M. (1996) *The Development of Language and Literacy*. London: Hodder and Stoughton.

Whyte, J. (1983) *Beyond the Wendy House: Sex-Role Stereotyping in Primary Schools*. York: Longman.

Williams, P. (1995) *Making Sense of Quality: A Review of Approaches to Quality in Early Childhood Services*. London: National Children's Bureau.

Winnicott, D.W. (1957) *The Child, the Family and the Outside World*. London: Penguin.

Winnicott, D.W. (1971) *Playing and Reality*. London: Routledge.

Wood, D. (1988) *How Children Think and Learn*. Oxford: Blackwell.

Wood, D., Bruner, J. and Ross, G. (1976) The role of tutoring in problem-solving. *Journal of Child Psychiatry and Psychology*, 17: 89–100.

Woodhead, M., Faulkner, D. and Littleton, K. (eds) (1988) *Cultural Worlds of Early Childhood*. London: Routledge.

Young-Bruehl, E. (1988) *Anna Freud*. London: Macmillan.

FURTHER READING

Bradley, B. (1989) *Visions of Infancy*. London: Polity Press.
Bredekamp, S. and Copple, C. (eds) (1997) *Developmentally Appropriate Practice in Early Childhood Programs*. Washington DC: National Association for the Education of Young Children.
Bronfenbrenner, U. (1979) *The Ecology of Human Development*. Cambridge, MA: Harvard University Press.
Bruner, J.S. (1972) The nature and uses of immaturity. *American Psychologist*, 27: 687–708.
Dunn, J. (1993) *Young Children's Close Relationships, Beyond Attachment*. London: Sage.
Edwards, C., Gandini, L. and Forman, G. (1994) *The Hundred Languages of Children. The Reggio Emilia Approach to Early Childhood Education*. NJ: Ablex Publishing.
Elfer, P. and Selleck, D. (1999) Children under three in nurseries: uncertainty as a creative factor in child observations. *European Journal*, 7 (1): 69–82.
Fein, G.G., Gariboldi, A. and Boni, R. (1993) The adjustment of infants and toddlers to group care: The first six months. *Early Childhood Research Quarterly*, 8 (1): 1–14.
Fein, G.G. (1995) Infants in group care: Patterns of despair and detachment. *Early Childhood Research Quarterly*, 10(3): 261–75.
Goldschmied, E. (1989) *Infants at Work*. London: National Children's Bureau (training video).
Goldschmied, E. and Hughes, A. (1992) *Heuristic Play with Objects*. London: National Children's Bureau (training video).
Greenberg, P. (1991) *Character Development. Encouraging Self-Esteem and Self-Discipline in Infants, Toddlers and Two Year Olds.*

Washington DC: National Association for the Education of Young Children.

Karmiloff-Smith, A. (1992) *Beyond Modularity. A Developmental Perspective on Cognitive Science*. Cambridge, MA. MIT Press.

Moss, P. and Pence, A. (eds) (1994) *Valuing Quality in Early Childhood Services. New Approaches to Defining Quality*. London: Paul Chapman.

Moyles, J. (ed) (1994) *The Excellence of Play*. Buckingham: Open University Press.

Schieffelin, B.B. and Ochs, E. (1987) *Language Socialisation Across Cultures*. Cambridge: Cambridge University Press.

Singer, E. (1998) Shared care for children, in M. Woodhead, D. Faulkner and K. Littleton (eds) *Cultural Worlds of Early Childhood*. London: Routledge.

INDEX

FROM BIRTH TO ONE
THE YEAR OF OPPORTUNITY

Maria Robinson

The first year of life is the year of opportunity. It is when the foundations for our emotional and social well being together with our motivation and ability to learn begin to be laid down by an ongoing interplay of physical, neurological and psychological processes.

Maria Robinson draws upon up to date research to illuminate this process and highlights the importance of understanding the meaning and influence of adult interactions, reactions and behaviour towards their child and the child's impact on the adult. She indicates how the outcomes of early experience can influence the direction of future development so providing insight into the potential reasons for children's behavioural responses.

The powerful nature of working with babies and young children is addressed in a separate section which encourages practitioners to reflect on how personal attitudes, beliefs and values can influence professional practice.

This fascinating book is a valuable resource for all early years practitioners including teachers, social workers and health visitors who wish to understand behaviour within a context of early developmental processes.

Contents
*Introduction – **Part one: Development in the first year** – Making connections: a perspective on development – Setting the scene: parents and parenting – Starting out: from birth to three months – From smiling to waving: 3 months–7 months – Peek a boo and where are you?: 7 months–12 months – Unhappy babies – **Part two: Reflections on professional practice and personal emotions** – The personal in the professional – When dreams go awry – The year of opportunity – References – Index.*

208pp   0 335 20895 9 (Paperback)   0 335 20896 7 (Hardback)